The Consultant's Guide to Success with 360 Degree Feedback

How to design and deliver bespoke 360 Degree Feedback that your clients will love

JO AYOUBI

To my mother, Dolores Ayoubi

For your unwavering love and support, and for always
being my number one fan

****

For consultants who do not have much experience designing, managing and delivering bespoke 360 degree feedback, this is an excellent primer. With input from experts - consultants who've been there, done that, got the t-shirt - this book provides pragmatic advice about the end to end process through stories and FAQs. Easy to read. Easy to implement. You'll be adding real value to your client organisations after one read!

Michelle Brailsford
Senior Partner, Jupiter Consulting Group

***

The Consultant's Guide to Success with 360 Degree Feedback is a condensed version of Jo Ayoubi's and Track Survey's extensive knowledge on all aspects of 360 degree processes, tools and feedback. It is a compact and comprehensive book packed full of all the information you need to know to get a successful 360 feedback process up and running. This unbiased view shares all the wonderful 'stuff' you get from 360 feedback plus the warts, giving a full and unadulterated view of all aspects of 360 giving clarity and understanding. Fabulous! A 'must' for any consultants, leaders, manager or organisation, considering 360 feedback.

Marie Smith
Owner, SUCCESSMITH

***

This book is a short, concise and well written introduction to the sometimes contentious subject of 360 Degree Feedback. It is clearly structured and presents a fair and balanced approach, presenting the case for and against the key issues identified and allowing the reader to consider options best suited to their own organisations and situations. I thought the discussion on bespoke or off the shelf solutions to be an excellent example of balance. The use of numerous expert comments and case studies added weight and interest to the points being made. By raising and then answering virtually all the very real questions raised by people considering using 360 degree feedback Jo showed her experience, understanding and command of her subject. I enjoyed and appreciated the book and many of the observations and stories told reflect my own experiences of 360 degree feedback.

Chris Fenney
Director and Co-Founder, Training Edge International Pte Ltd

***

How I wish this book had been around a few years ago! Full of useful insights and advice it should be on the 'essential reading' list for any consultant advising organisations on the effective use of 360 feedback.

Una McGarvie
Owner, Insight In Change

Table of Contents

Introduction

About This Book

My friends tell me that being a Human Resources or Training Consultant is great. "You get to work with interesting people," they say, "in cool organisations that are at the leading edge of performance and development. Not only that," they continue, "but you get paid a fortune, and you even get decide when to work and when to take a day off!"

If you're a consultant you know that most of the above is true (except the last two). We do love our work, but our friends don't always see the competitors, the late night working, the tight deadlines, and the challenge of finding new ways of engaging with clients.

With a background in organisational development, I have been designing, managing and delivering 360 Degree Feedback through my company, Track Surveys Limited (www.tracksurveys.co.uk) since the year 2000. I have worked as both an independent consultant, and within a wider team of consultants, and subsequently as business development director at the head of Track Surveys. I believe that 360 Degree Feedback is a fantastic tool, not only for organisations to be able to improve performance, but also for consultants to develop their client relationships and add tangible value to those relationships.

I've also learned that 360 is a complex, multi-layered process that needs a structured approach, meticulous preparation and seamless delivery to succeed. This can seem daunting to the consultant or consultancy team whose expertise is in HR, training and development, talent management or succession planning.

Hence, I saw a need for a clearly written, jargon-free guide covering the key questions that consultants ask when thinking about using 360 Degree Feedback, and that's why I wrote this book. In writing it, I have used my own experience over 13 years, and the most common questions I get asked about 360. I have also included interviews and observations from highly experienced consultants, along with case studies, references and items from other sources.

Although this book is aimed at external consultants, in business on their own or in partnership with others, much of the information is just as relevant if you work within an organisation in people performance and development.

So whether you're thinking about using 360 for the first time, or you've used it before but are looking at refreshing and revitalizing your 360 programmes, the goal of this book is to give you some ideas and nuggets that will simplify your work and maximise its value.

Who's who: Terminology

As this book aimed at consultants, I use 'clients' to refer to the project leader, sponsor or decision-maker within the client organisation. If you are an internal consultant, this will refer to your internal clients and stakeholders.

I've referred to the people in client organisations who are receiving 360 Degree Feedback as 'learners', to cover as many 360 feedback scenarios as possible.

The colleagues who are invited to, or who actually, give feedback to learners, are referred to as 'respondents'.

I have used 'Coach' or 'Debriefer' to refer to a person whose specific role is to debrief the learner through their individual 360 Degree Feedback report. This might be an internal or external coach or mentor, an HR or training professional, or the individual's line manager, if appropriate.

How this book is structured

I've structured this book into six (6) sections, each covering the most frequently asked questions about the design, implementation and use of 360 Degree Feedback. Within each section, I have used a Question and Answer format, as well as the interviews with experts, and case studies. You can read the book all the way through, or you may prefer to dip into areas that interest you, or that are relevant to you right now.

From this book, you will learn how to create and deliver a successful 360 Degree Feedback programme that will engage your learners, help them with their personal and professional growth, and impress your clients.

I hope you enjoy it!

Jo Ayoubi

www.tracksurveys.co.uk

November 2013

Important!

I've assumed a basic level of understanding about 360 Degree Feedback and the concepts behind it. If you're not sure how the basics work, please go to Appendix 1, which will give you a quick overview.

PART 1

Adding Value with 360 Degree Feedback

As consultants working in the field of people development and performance, we know that feedback is essential.

... EXPERT COMMENT ...

Peter Honey, *Occupational Psychologist, Author & Management Trainer*

"It does seem to me that feedback is essential. Do you know the experiment with dartboards? It's a wonderful example of how feedback works. I've demonstrated it and it does actually illustrate the point, so you might like to try it.

You take someone who's pretty good at hitting a standard dartboard more or less where they aim, to get triple or double 20.

You let them take aim in their normal way, with no interference at all from anyone. As soon as they've thrown the dart, you whip a tray up in front of their eyes so they can't see where it has landed - no feedback. They've been deprived of the feedback you normally get when you throw a dart, that is, knowing where the dart has landed, and then making some minute adjustment on your next throw to get closer to the target.

Over the space of, say, 12 throws in this way, they'll get noticeably worse at hitting their target. They will make all their normal adjustments, but without feedback, their performance will decline.

That seems to me to be a simple demonstration of how absolutely essential feedback is, just for sustaining performance, never mind improving it.

So I say, 'no feedback, no learning'."

• • • • • •

360 Degree Feedback takes the basic concept of feedback to another level. By incorporating:

• Self-review and reflection by the learner,

• Feedback from multiple observers with different relationships to the learner,
• Structure and consistency of feedback themes,
• Links to the organisation's people development and performance strategies,

360 can offer a richer and more integrated way of using feedback to benefit the individual and the organisation.

360 Degree Feedback provides the Learner with feedback from Senior colleagues, Peers, and Subordinates (Reports), as well as an opportunity to self-assess, as shown in the diagram below.

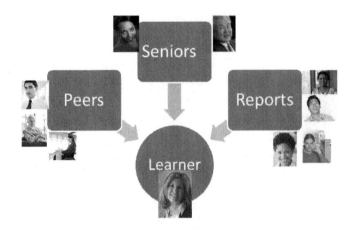

The British Psychological Society summarizes the broad benefits of 360 Degree Feedback[i] as follows:

• Increased understanding of the behaviours required to improve both individual and organisational effectiveness
• More focused development activities, built around the skills and competencies required for successful organisational performance
• Increased involvement of people at all levels of the organisation
• Increased individual ownership for self-development and learning

• Increased familiarity with the implications of cultural or strategic change

1. How can 360 Degree Feedback add value to my client's training, development and coaching programmes?

Most professionals think of 360 Degree Feedback as a tool to help with individual coaching, training and development. In this context, the 360 helps learners to become aware of how they are seen by their work colleagues, and pinpoints areas of strength, as well behaviours they should modify. A good 360 can be a springboard for improving individual learning, skills and behaviours. It is, therefore, a very important starting point for creating a development plan for individual learners that is tailored around their personal activities and behaviours.

As a consultant, 360 Degree Feedback gives you a toolkit to support the development and performance of individual learners in your client organisations.

... EXPERT COMMENT ...

Clive Bradley, Managing Director, The Development Matrix

"I can count on one hand the amount of times that a client has said, '...and we'd like to use the 360 Degree Feedback.' Clients talk about how they'd like do some development, and improve the individual learner, but in general, it's me as the consultant that suggests we start with a benchmark. That benchmark is created by a 360 tool. There may be other tools and development items the client suggests, but the most consistent thing for me is the 360 tool. Other things come and go around it, but it's the 360 that I put first and foremost into the conversation.

Now if we utilize the 360 correctly, it will give the individual complete feedback on their current skills, including the good, the bad and the indifferent, from their peers, their subordinates, and manager. This then gives us a good basis to start the dialogue around what their starting position looks like, and where they want to go."

. . . . . .

2. How can 360 Degree Feedback benefit my clients in a strategic way?

Whilst organisations benefit from individual improvements, 360 can offer additional value as a strategic development and performance tool. Structured individual development plans can lead the way into identifying common training needs within groups or teams. Group 360 reports can be brilliant for team facilitation and performance planning, and the 360 can provide valuable data for identifying, tracking and developing learners on talent programmes.

Moreover, 360s that are specifically designed for the organisation, that is, bespoke 360s, can form the basis for defining the outcomes of a behaviour change programme, and then for measuring the success of those outcomes on an ongoing basis. In fact, the very process of creating a bespoke 360 Degree Feedback tool can really help to put words and actions around the objectives of the change programme.

. . . EXPERT COMMENTS . . .

Sue Oliver, Business and Coaching Psychologist, Business Psychology for Leaders

"What I love about 360 Degree Feedback is that it's not just 'let's run some one-to-one sessions and look at individual development', although it is that too.

It's actually part of the more strategic application of a management development programme. In this case, 360 can be linked to the training and development strategy for the organisation. So we could have a group of 50 managers and from the 360, we can see that they are a strong team. But we can also see that there appears to be a delegation problem in the overall team. The 360 feedback will allow us as an organisation to then look at the results and ask ourselves 'Are we providing the right environment and support to let these managers delegate? Maybe not."

. . .

Clive Bradley, Managing Director, The Development Matrix

"In my experience, what learners tend to do when they get their 360 Degree Feedback report is to go to page 4 and page 9 (or the equivalent). Page 4 is the summary of scores and page 9 is the individual comments that respondents have made about them. For the learner, it's initially 'let's cut to the chase'; this means that they may miss the subtleties. But it's the subtleties that really matter, and allow them either to buy in and accept the feedback messages, or to challenge those messages with a bit of rigour.

Quite often, in my experience with senior teams, learners will say, 'I've heard all this before. We don't need to go through this process. We are all old, wise and experienced enough to be able to have these conversations with one another without the need for hiding behind the 360 process.' Of course, I will then say, 'I think you've missed the point! If you already know these things, why haven't you done them differently up to now?!'

The 360 Degree Feedback gives you so much more ability to change the organisation, because an individual's actions and behaviours at the board level may well influence the behaviours and actions of their subordinates and their teams. This then has a direct correlation to the performance of the organisation, the results they get, and the culture within which they operate. When you explain it from that point of view, as a bigger picture, the board and senior management will say, 'Okay, I get it."

. . . . . .

. . . *IN THE NEWS* . . .

360 degree feedback valued by Sunday Times Top 100 Best Places to Work

"One Sunday Times company said: "Eight years ago the company was lacklustre and underperforming in the sector. We are now ahead of the sector and are in it for the long term. We carry out a collective 360 process, where we listen to what our employees say and act upon it." *(Web Link: bit.ly/InTheNews1)*

· · · · · ·

3. In what specific situations can 360 Degree Feedback add value?

The one-word answer to this question is 'change'. People working in organisations most need structured feedback in times of change, whether that is in individual terms, such as changing roles or getting promoted, when they need to manage and motivate others, or when they are being called upon to change the organisation and use new behaviours are needed to achieve that change.

At these critical change points, an awareness of one's skills, behaviours and capabilities, measured against the requirements of the new role, is the first step in the learner understanding what they will need to do to progress – or indeed, what strengths they already have to do so.

Surprisingly, a survey published in 2009[ii] showed that only one quarter of the companies surveyed were judged to be 'good' (as opposed to fair or poor) at helping people transition from 'individual contributor' status to manager roles.

... EXPERT COMMENTS ...

Clive Bradley, Managing Director, The Development Matrix

"For any organisation, there's no point in promising the world to your customers, stakeholder and employees, talking about stretch targets and strategic intents, if you have no idea whether you have the resources to achieve them. If your strategy is not aligned with the resources that you've got available, then it's going to fail. A good analogy is: I'm driving a car and decide I want to drive at 140 mph, but I have a problem if I have no idea whether the car can actually do that speed!

So for the client organisation, 360 Degree Feedback can be a means of understanding the resources available to them, so they can then make an informed decision about their people performance and development strategy. The way I explain it to my clients is that we need to get a benchmark in place, and one of the key things for creating that benchmark is decent dialogue around the 360 Degree Feedback and how to use it to best effect."

. . .

Sue Thompson, Project Coordinator, Eliesha Training

"Clients need to have a look at where their people are before they start a major training or development programme, because what learners think of as being their own developmental needs are not always the case, or the issue the organisation needs to deal with. It's one thing sitting down in the annual appraisal with employees and saying to them, 'Okay, what do you think you need to do in the next year?' But if you haven't got any hard evidence around that, it makes it that conversation much more difficult. This is true particularly in the environment that we're in now, where resources are limited and budgets for learning and development just aren't there anymore. So it's vital to get right to the heart of what each individual employee needs to learn and improve.

Therefore, the organisation will clearly benefit by using its competency and behavioural framework, which can then be

25

tracked by the 360 Degree Feedback, and so relate the feedback exactly to what the employee needs in order to be able to do their job more successfully."

. . .

Peter Honey, *Occupational Psychologist, Author & Management Trainer*

"Senior managers are very good examples of people who are often deprived of information; either they are fed with heavily laundered information or no information reaches them at all, which I think is how they can so easily get out of touch. In fact, it's impossible for senior managers to really know what's going on. It's very likely that they're going to be lacking feedback, which creates a serious problem."

• • • • • •

4. What's the difference between an off-the-shelf and a bespoke 360 Degree Feedback tool, and which is better?

There are many off-the-shelf 360 Degree Feedback questionnaires on the market; many of these are excellent. These types of tools are based on a particular model of leadership, management or role. The same set of competencies and statements (or questions) is used with a large number of learners.

These off-the-shelf tools are great for individual coaching and career development where the coach and the learner are focused on the learner's own development journey, without specific reference to their organisational goals. So the choice of an off-the-shelf questionnaire will depend on the preference of the coach, the role and aspirations of the learner, and the overall context of the coaching activity (e.g. management, leadership, EQ).

Bespoke 360 Degree Feedback is an altogether different animal. A bespoke 360 Degree Feedback can be built around the organisation's own competencies, key capabilities, leadership frameworks and values. It adds value by being able to define the behaviours and the skills that people need specifically in the organisation, and then to measure these.

For example, a consultant may be asked to create a development programme for leaders or partners in a law firm. That development programme is based very specifically on what that law firm wants to achieve – what its goals are – and therefore the behaviours it wants to define for its people. Therefore, a bespoke 360 would be a very powerful tool for creating a common understanding of what leadership means, and looks like, in their firm – and what is expected of their people.

... EXPERT COMMENT ...

Jane Beirne, *Learning and Development Director, Jane Beirne Learning Solutions Limited*

"I think that the bespoke 360 Degree Feedback is really useful in looking at cultural fit to make sure that the language and the values of the organisation are reflected in the questions. To me, the 360 reflects the values at work within that organisation and therefore, what's important to that organisation might be quite different to another.

Therefore, how people are being assessed will be in the context of that organisation. That's really where you get the benefit of the bespoke 360 - working closely within the parameters of that organisation."

• • • • • •

... CASE STUDY ...

A Strategic 360 for a New Merged Group of Companies

We recently had a call from a client whose organisation has been acquiring smaller businesses in its sector, where it has a long history of success and a trusted brand. As part of the integration process, a set of leadership skills and values had been developed

27

for the new, larger organisation, and all managers were to participate in a programme to develop those skills and embed those values. However the provider of the development programme was only able to offer the client an off-the-shelf 360 Degree Feedback to support the programme.

For the client, a bespoke 360 that stated the leadership behaviours and the shared values, in a common language, was critical to the success of the integration programme. We are now working with them to develop a 360 which will then be used all around the client's organisation to develop a common corporate and a set of shared values and behaviours. Additionally the online questionnaires and reports will be branded to match the integrated organisation's branding, even down to the font size and the colours in the report!

· · · · · ·

... EXPERT COMMENT ...

Sue Oliver, *Business and Coaching Psychologist, Business Psychology for Leaders*

"In a situation where I haven't done 360 Degree Feedback with the client before, I have to think quite carefully about what will work for them. A good example would be a small manufacturing firm, with only 100 staff, and that doesn't do performance appraisals that well, but who want to change. In that case, I would ideally love to help them find some proper competencies and do 360 based around those, but I know that's not going to work for them at this point.

So in that kind of situation, the off-the-shelf 360 would work really well, not just for budget reasons, but also because you sometimes need to do this kind of work in baby steps. This is the consultant's dilemma: you don't want to sell the client a Rolls Royce when all they need is a Ford. You might scare them off, so it's important not to oversell.

So as long as I don't go against my ethics and my values, what I would suggest to the client in this situation is, 'How about if we just think about three or four key competencies of managers in general. Here is what the research has shown us...' (it could be managing self, managing others, managing communication, managing the business, for example).

That's when I think an off-the-shelf is perfect. The client doesn't need anything more complicated. They're not used to behavioural language or observation. They don't know what getting feedback is, so you've got to make it simple, but at the same time, professional and effective."

$\bullet$ $\bullet$ $\bullet$ $\bullet$ $\bullet$ $\bullet$

5. How can a bespoke 360 Degree Feedback work as an effective organisational change tool for my clients?

A bespoke 360 Degree Feedback (as described in 4 above) can be a remarkably flexible and strategic tool when it is designed to align with the organisation's competencies, key capabilities, values and performance metrics.

We have worked with clients using 360 Degree Feedback to support a wide variety of HR and Training and Development activities, including:

- Assessing current management and leadership skills
- Evaluating potential for management and leadership
- Talent identification and tracking
- Strategic capability assessment and tracking
- Development planning for performance appraisal
- Total Quality Management and Lean[iii] programmes
- Investors In People[iv]: defining and tracking current and future progress

... IN THE NEWS ...

Google methodologies for business success

"We measure people every 90 days. We get 360 degree feedback on people every 180 days and that feedback is published to the whole company. People want reality. Ninety per cent of the rewards end up going to ten percent of the people." - *John*

Herlihy, Google VP of Global Ad Operations (Web Link: bit.ly/InTheNews3)

HRD 2010: Cadbury introduces '720-degree' feedback

"Not content with 360-degree feedback for her new leadership development programme, *Sarah Smith, head of the L&D centre of excellence for Cadbury UK&I*, went a step further – "720-degree" feedback includes input from a leader's family and friends, as well as business colleagues and direct reports." *(Web Link: bit.ly/InTheNews4)*

· · · · · ·

... EXPERT COMMENT ...

Jane Beirne, Learning and Development Director, Jane Beirne Learning Solutions Limited

"Although for me, 360 Degree Feedback is still a very personal process, it can also be a strategic organisational change tool. If a member of a senior team, or any group of people in the organisation, is going through the 360 Degree Feedback process, one of the by-products is that they now have a platform to discuss their development and their needs in a more open forum. It encourages more open and frank conversation and an environment that actually supports development, by pulling teams through high levels of challenge and high levels of support.

For example, if it were a line manager who had already been through the 360 Degree Feedback process, then he or she would be far more proactive in their support and challenge of their reports, and also of their peer groups. So while 360 works as an individual tool, where everyone in a group has modelled and demonstrated the 360 behaviours, and has been facilitated and encouraged to talk about their learnings as a result, it becomes integrated into the cultural piece. Therefore, the benefit is that you get a much more open and frank exchange."

· · · · · ·

... IN THE NEWS ...

Strategic Management Development across Europe

(Reported in the Sunday Times, October 2006)

Fujitsu Services is one of the leading IT service companies in Europe, the Middle East and Africa. It employs more than 21,000 people in over 20 countries in a £2.4 billion business headquartered in London.

In 2006, Fujitsu Services launched the Fujitsu Management Academy, involving 2,200 managers based in 13 countries who took part in a dedicated management development programme, delivered in 11 different languages.

With this purpose-designed scheme, Fujitsu was able to employ its own expert consultants, devise its own syllabus and focus on turning its technically-oriented people into rounded people managers.

Before tackling the second module, all the managers participate in the bespoke 360 Degree Feedback that has been designed to measure the people management skills that the programme will develop. Track Surveys, a company which specialises in the 360 Degree Feedback process used to assess managers, designed and delivered the programme across all the countries, and in all the languages of the learners and their respondents.

"The feedback from the tool was excellent, well done and managed outstandingly," said a senior leader. "Participants were brought together in a group that didn't include immediate colleagues, so we were able to discuss issues arising from the feedback in a secure and safe environment.

The feedback I received was useful and insightful and has led me to reassess and refresh my approach to people management. I look forward to doing the 360 degree feedback at the end of module three to see how much things have changed."

To get this message out and chase the vision we need a reputation programme and a people development programme to

31

enable all employees to share a common language, management behaviours and attitude," said the programme director.

. . . . . .

6. How can 360 Degree Feedback be strategic for me as a consultant?

As we have discussed, a bespoke 360 can be a brilliant tool for defining the outcomes, behaviours and skills that an organisation wants to develop in its people. The 360 is particularly useful for defining hard-to-measure, behavioural outcomes in management or leadership programmes.

By building a strategic 360 Degree Feedback for your client, that aligns with your programme, and that measures the changes you will deliver, you can prove the return on your programme and the value of what you provide to your client.

The 360 can also give you great data that you can take to your client, prompting further discussions and analysis, identifying further training needs, highlighting themes and predicting future requirements – overall, giving you a good reason to keep talking and working with your client – and demonstrating your value and expertise.

Using the right tools that give you a high level of flexibility in design and reporting, 360 Degree Feedback can provide lots more opportunities to introduce new concepts, training, development and talent programmes based on that 360. The group aggregated 360 results, for example, may highlight some additional coaching or training needs that you can then provide to your client. It's a great tool for opening up new opportunities hence it can be very strategic for your consulting business.

Interestingly, only two-fifths of organisations surveyed in the Chartered Institute of Personnel and Development's (CIPD) 2013 survey said that they used 360 Degree Feedback to evaluate management and leadership skills of their employees[v]. There is therefore a wide area of opportunity for consultants to help organisations use 360 as a strategic development tool.

... *EXPERT COMMENTS* ...

Jane Beirne, Learning and Development Director, Jane Beirne Learning Solutions Limited

"360 Degree Feedback has been a great tool to use with my clients. It opens dialogue and it gives a different focus from just a one-to-one coaching session. It certainly brings a different dynamic. The professional 360 Degree Feedback reports that each learner receives are very useful. The feedback can be correlated with other tools that you might have used as part of your service. From the credibility and professional point of view, it supports the services and offers that I can provide to my clients."

. . .

Julian Hammond, Director, TIPS for Good Management

"On some occasions, the 360 Degree Feedback results gave us more opportunity for one-to-one coaching of our clients' learners.

For example, on one particular management development programme, we had created and agreed on eight management competencies with the client. Each individual wouldn't necessarily need to work on all the competencies, so we used the 360 Degree Feedback interviews to 'cherry pick' the things each learner really needed from the course. In that way, each learner came in to the course with their own personal plan. In practice, this meant that for one person, the session on time management might be of particular importance, for somebody else it might be leading people, developing teams or process improvement. In this, way we were able to provide a tailored programme for each learner, which is much more effective than everyone having to learn things they don't need.

I've also seen it happen where, following the post course, one-to-one 360 Degree Feedback debriefing with a learner, further development opportunities become apparent. An example would be leadership, which had only been at an introductory level on the management development programme. However several learners wanted to know more about the subject as a result of their 360 Degree Feedback. This then gave rise to further discussions with the client about follow-up programmes or coaching support in the business."

. . . . . .

7. Can I use 360 Degree Feedback to evaluate the quality of our client development programmes?

It's typically difficult to run effective training evaluations at the Kirkpatrick Levels 3 and 4 (transfer of behaviour change to the workplace and results for the business, respectively). That's because those levels are about observation and measurement on behaviours in the workplace. For this reason, 360 Degree Feedback is one of the few tools that can assess the effect of training at those levels, by using it as a 'before-and-after' measurement for client interactions, leadership, teamwork, talent and other behavioural change activities.

. . . EXPERT COMMENTS . . .

Sue Thompson, *Project Coordinator, Eliesha Training*

"Ultimately, it's being able to show the benefit of what we do and the return on investment, which really matters. That's why when a major client in the public sector embarked upon a two-year development programme, the learners first completed the 360 Degree Feedback exercise, creating metrics to inform the programme. At the end of two years, we ran another 360 to see how far they had progressed.

That's one of the reasons we've kept on winning this work – we have had this client's business now for about six years, and that's because we do offer them something that is different to the other providers.

Our experience is that this approach works, and we use this as an example when we speak to new clients."

. . .

Julian Hammond, *Director, TIPS for Good Management*

"An example of being able to measure ROI (return on investment) of 360 Degree Feedback occurred with a client who had a number of issues with what they initially described as 'poor time management'.

Each month they would have literally hundreds of meetings throughout the organisation. So we presented some techniques and methods to sharpen up their meeting practice, knowing they would get some real tangible benefit in the business and be able to measure it. Before the training commenced, we ran a bespoke 360 feedback which identified their behaviours and included a method of rating their effectiveness. Approximately three months after the training, we interviewed the learners again using exactly the same questions and repeated the 360 rating exercise.

The results clearly demonstrated the difference before and after the training intervention and, for the vast majority of learners, had improved by the second round of 360 Degree Feedback. This improvement could be expressed in terms of financial value to the business."

. . . . . .

. . . CASE STUDY . . .

Measuring the Impact of a Global Management Development Programme

PLAN is one of the largest international development agencies in the world, focused on helping children in developing countries. The organisation is growing by 20% yearly and has nearly 8000 employees and 60,000 volunteers, most of whom are in the field making a difference to the lives of more than 1.5 million children and their families.

In 2004, as part of a global management training strategy, a comprehensive Global Training Needs Analysis was initiated which evaluated staff in 37 countries. The Learning and Development team analysed 30 urgent development needs and prioritised them in 4 key disciplines:

  • Developing as a Leader: e.g. 'Strategic Thinking' and 'Giving Direction'
  • Working with People: e.g. 'Nurturing and Developing Others'
  • Communication Skills: e.g. 'Negotiating and Influencing'
  • Business Skills: e.g. 'Building Partnerships', 'Resource Mobilisation', and 'Participation Skills'

A major design project ensued, resulting in a partnership including PLAN and a number of specialist training design and delivery providers. A key element of the programme was a bespoke 360 Degree Feedback programme that measured the programme participants before and after their learning activities.

The programme was extremely successful, and the 360 Degree Feedback demonstrated this – the Towards Maturity Case Study[vi] describes this in detail. The 360 Degree Feedback demonstrated how much of a change there was in the management behaviours of the learners following the programme. The line managers of the learners, in particular, observed an average of 45% improvement across the behaviours being developed. Highlights included Leadership & Management and Decision Making improving by 61%, and Leading Change improving by 54%.

8. How can I link or combine 360 Degree Feedback data with other data to create new insights for our clients?

With the ability to access and report data in different ways, another exciting opportunity for offering insights to your client is in combining the 360 with other data, helping the client to make better informed decisions.

Data that can be combined creatively include basic human resources data such as absence, sickness, qualifications, etc. (which abound in most organisations), data produced by processes such as performance review and 360 Degree Feedback, satisfaction and engagement data, exit data and performance analytics.[vii]

When the 360 Degree Feedback is run using online data capture, your 360 management system should be able to help you to combine the results with other data and create new insights for your clients.

... CASE STUDY ...

Identifying Leadership Potential and Succession

An organisation in the professional services sector was looking for insights on leadership potential and whether they had the people with the right leadership skills to be able to take on critical roles in the upcoming years. This was a strategic imperative, and critical in a highly competitive and fast-changing professional services sector.

By combining 360 feedback data, development centre ratings and other data, the client was able to rate each candidate on a scale of readiness for a leadership role.

They were then able to identify candidates who were ready for a leadership role, those who needed more development, and critically, people who would not be put forward for future development at this high level. The information helped the organisation to target its efforts in the most strategic and cost-effective way.

For more examples of the kinds of data that can be combined in this way, see the 'Turn Talent into Real Information' article in Harvard Business Review Blog Network.[viii]

• • • • • •

9. What if a client wants to do 360 Degree Feedback, but doesn't know what culture they are trying to enhance or

create? Can a bespoke 360 help them answer that question?

The actual task of designing a 360 really forces the organisation to think about what they want people to do differently, beyond the 'headline' behaviours and value statements.

The creation or change of organisation's culture is a complex project, but one of the keys to creating change is making the changes relevant to how individuals, teams and managers do their job every day. By doing this, general aspirational statements are then broken down into observable, measurable actions, through the bespoke 360 design.

The consultant can help the organisation to state and test the changes it wants to see: what they look like, who sees them, and when.

... EXPERT COMMENT ...

Sue Mills, Principal Client Relationship Manager, Eliesha Training

"What we try to do is to fit the 360 Degree Feedback into other interventions, making sure that what we're delivering is right for the client. It's really important that we work with the client to help them consider what they want their outcomes to be before they embark on 360 Degree Feedback.

Often organisations can think, 'We've used 360 in appraisal and development - that's a great way to get people motivated,' but they don't know what they want learners to get out of it and they don't understand how best to (make it) work for them."

. . . . . .

10. Are there certain types of business or sectors in particular that benefit from 360 Degree Feedback?

You can run 360 Degree Feedback in every sector, especially since it's now possible to use technology to contact people and complete 360s over the internet, on mobile phones and tablets –

so you can include everyone in the process, no matter where they are in the world.

Traditionally, professional services like banking and accountancy were early adopters of 360 Degree Feedback. Now banking and financial sector companies in particular are seeing the importance of developing a consistent culture and values that are measurable and assessable at an individual level. What makes 360 ideal for regulated industries is that it can include bespoke organisational elements, together with industry standards or regulatory items, hence providing both an internal measure for behaviours and an external measure for compliance.

However, other sectors are also starting to think about the benefits of the 360 model. For example, we have designed and run 360s for law firms, which traditionally did not use this technique. But because of the challenges they are now facing (with increased competition and changes in the business rules), many firms are now picking up on using 360 to assess and build non-technical skills, and thereby increase their competitive advantage.

Another sector that is now embracing 360 is retail. It may come as a surprise but we now work with some very large UK retail clients, which are looking to compete on the quality of their people and working relationships, as well as their customer service.

Sectors that we are actively working with on using 360 Degree Feedback include:

- Law
- Accounting
- Finance
- Insurance
- Retail
- Healthcare
- Housing associations
- Manufacturing

11. At what level does 360 Degree Feedback work best: junior, middle or senior?

Although 360 Degree Feedback is most often used with senior executives, it works equally well to support the development of both junior employees and middle-ranking managers. Provided the objectives for the 360 are clear, and the questions have been designed based on the correct skill and competency level for the learner group, the benefits of the 360 feedback can be significant, whatever the age or experience of the learners.

Where the differences lie are in the positioning of the 360, how it is communicated and how the feedback is debriefed, as different learner group will have different levels of experience and preferences in dealing with the feedback they receive.

. . . EXPERT COMMENT . . .

Clive Bradley, Managing Director, The Development Matrix

"Graduates are much more accepting of 360 Degree Feedback. Senior people are sometimes initially dismissive of it, not necessarily because of what the tool could do for them, but more around their understanding of its benefits. Their initial view might be, 'I've done that before, I've seen it before, it's not going to do anything more for me.' However, if you can couple the 360 Degree Feedback with their objectives, and within the coaching relationship, they start to get it.

Graduates don't necessarily go through the same thought process. They are excited, they are accepting of feedback and they are thrilled when they get to open it and read it; it's like a present!

However, graduates, in my experience, fall a lot harder if they get some unexpected critical feedback. This is because they tend to 'personalise' the comments, and take them more to heart. More senior people don't personalise the feedback so much; they take the feedback with a pinch of salt because they have the experience and the confidence to admit, for example, '...not everybody likes my style.'

Graduates can be more easily hurt and say 'This person thinks I'm no good' or 'This person thinks I'm failing'. You then have to coach them through this carefully, saying, 'They're not saying you're no good, it's just that they are saying you need to learn to deal with ambiguity better,' or whatever the feedback said. You have to explain it and position it differently for them."

. . . . . .

12. What other development tools can work well with 360 Degree Feedback?

There are many tools that consultants use as part of their training, development coaching and facilitation. Psychometric tools are often used alongside 360 Degree Feedback to give a further level of insight to the learner.

360 Degree Feedback is often likened to psychometric assessments and in some ways, they are similar. However, the key differences between 360 and psychometric tools are:

Psychometric tools tend to focus on personality traits and preferences, whilst 360s are generally based on observable actions.

Psychometric tools are based on the perceptions or judgments of the individual learner only, whilst 360 combines the view of many colleagues who can offer diverse observations.

In general, people do not change much in their personality or ways of looking at the world (as measured by psychometric instruments). Specific behaviours, measured in the 360 tool, can be more readily changed, where the learner is willing to change and is supported to do so.

... EXPERT COMMENT ...

Jane Beirne, *Learning and Development Director, Jane Beirne Learning Solutions Limited*

"I use Myers-Briggs (Type Indicator) quite extensively to give people an insight into themselves. I also use 360 Degree Feedback to give them a starting point.

So with the MBTI, the learners will have looked at their preferred communication style, and considered that in relation to how they interact with other people. This is then followed up by presenting the conceptions of other people through the 360, and linking this with the messages from the MBTI.

So it's useful to work in tandem in that way, as a benchmarking process. Because I've probably used 360 Degree Feedback with learners initially, we might look to revisit that in 6-12 months' time, again depending on where they are in their development."

• • • • • •

Another tool which is often used alongside 360 Degree Feedback is the Johari Window, which most consultants will be familiar with. It helps the learner to think about their unknown strengths, as well as blind spots, and to understand that the 360 information is there to help them fill in those blind spots.

... CASE STUDY ...

A Consultant's Story (as told by Barry Sampson, Co-Founder and Director, Onlignment)

"One thing that I do have filed away is an appraisal of mine from 1997. My career up to that point was entirely in retail. I had been a retail manager for a petrol company, running various different sites in the south of London. I then worked for an off-licence chain where I ran a couple of community-type off-licenses and then a big wine store. I then went to work for a newsagents', as a store manager and relief manager, trouble-shooting issues in difficult stores. With the newsagents, I moved up to Scotland and ran one of the biggest stores in the country. With that experience you'd think I would have been confident that I knew what I was doing.

Then I got a job with a supermarket. So I went from what was the biggest store in Scotland for the newsagents, to what was a fairly low turnover supermarket, but I couldn't get it right. I successfully completed my induction, then they let me loose in the store, but I couldn't achieve the results; sales were dropping, shrinkage figures were going up, I just couldn't get it right.

42

It was after my appraisal at six months that my manager said in his written summary, 'Barry is a good person but if he carries on the way he is, he'll end up leaving.' He said, 'I'm not threatening you, and I'm not going to sack you, but you know that it's not working and I think if you carry on, you're just going to leave.' I went away and I thought, 'he's right, something's not working,' and really, that was the choice - am I going to try and do what it is I need to change or am I going to leave?

I went to some other store managers who were known as good performers and said, 'Can you come and have a look? Come and spend some time with me.' In a short time (it was only about 3 or 4 weeks), it suddenly became very obvious what it was I was doing wrong. I was trying to run what was a very complex business with the same mind-set I used to run something that was bigger, but much simpler. There was a difference between running a business where most of what we sold were cards, books, stationery, newspapers and magazines, to selling very low margin foodstuffs which had an equally short shelf life.

It worked well enough that by the end of that year I was running two stores and they were both twice the size of the store I previously run. I got that opportunity because I learned how to do things the right way, but that was only because there was a feedback process and someone was willing to be tough.

The supermarket was also the first place that 360 became part of my life. They had gone through a massive culture change. The board had realised that things were not going well and recognised that they needed help. They brought in consultants who told them that 'the problem is you haven't got a clue what your customers want and you haven't got a clue what your staff want'.

So, they had a choice, do nothing or change. They opted for radical change, and I joined the organisation just after this process had started. They were very focused on the customer, and very focused on employees. 360 Degree Feedback was key to achieving the latter.

As a store manager, my bonus had four parts to it, equally staked at 25%. One part was sales, one was profit, and together they contributed up to 50% of the bonus. The other half of the bonus was equally split between customer satisfaction scores and the staff element of your 360 feedback.

I think the 360 was really useful for me because it helped me, as a manager, to understand what the needs of my people were, because they had a really simple way of telling me when things weren't going right. People want accountability, people want clear objectives. When I first went in, I was 'being a manager'. I was managing staff, I was making decisions, and I was trying to figure out what to do. What 360 helped me do was rely on my team. By the time I was running the two stores, I rarely had to make operational decisions, as that was done by the department supervisors.

360 Degree Feedback is key to helping you understand what's going well and what's not going so well."

PART 2

Creating Engaging and Professional 360 Degree Feedback

1. Can I build a 360 Degree Feedback tool using competency frameworks?

Competency frameworks[ix] can be a very good basis for building a bespoke 360 Degree Feedback tool, by including competencies that are already familiar and specific to the organisation, and used for other purposes, such as recruitment and performance management.

In addition, many organisations will have spent a lot of time and effort (and cost) in developing their competency frameworks, leadership models or values and ethics models, and as a consultant it is a good idea to be aware if these exist, and, if possible, to incorporate them into your 360 design.

We would recommend, as much as possible, keeping the competency headings and using the framework statements (or values) as the basis for your 360 questions. These can then be tested and validated by appropriate stakeholders in the business, and modified as required.

2. Which works best, quantitative or qualitative feedback?

Quantitative 360 Degree Feedback is the response to a structured set of statements using a rating scale. The rating scale gives the respondent a very specific way of reporting on their observations of the learner's actions.

Here is an example of how an individual learner's capabilities have been ranked (from highest to lowest) based on their colleagues' 360 Degree Feedback. The learner's own self rating score is shown for comparison.

This chart enables you to compare your highest rated capabilities and your lowest rated capabilities as rated by your Reviewers. You can also see your Self-review ratings compared with the average of all your Reviewer ratings.

The benefits of using a rating scale and quantitative feedback are:

> • Consistency of theme
> By rating specific statements or questions (also known as 'items'), the learner and respondents are directed to think about those particular behaviours. The ratings can then be compared, (learner with respondents responses, respondent groups with each other), to get a clear, all-round view of how that person performs in those specific areas.
>
> • Key organisational capabilities
> The structured 360 allows everyone engaging with the process to think consistently about the key capabilities, skills and values that are important to the organisation. This helps to embed those capabilities as part of the culture of the organisation, and reinforce their importance in terms of performance and development.
>
> • Data on group strengths and development needs
> Where the feedback is structured and consistent, the organisation will have clear data on, not only learner, but also group, departmental and regional training needs. Similarly, there will be clear indicators to support decisions on leadership development, talent management and succession planning.

The disadvantage of quantitative feedback alone, as opposed to qualitative feedback, is that ratings alone do not provide a context or further information about the respondent's observations, and it is harder for the learner and their debriefer to interpret the meaning of the feedback ratings.

Qualitative feedback consists of free-text information provided by the learner and their respondents. Unlike quantitative feedback, qualitative feedback is prompted by open questions, such as "How could your colleague become a better leader?" or "What are your colleague's strengths as a manager?"

The advantage of qualitative feedback over ratings is that it is context specific. Because the feedback is in the form of examples or stories from respondents, it can be more specific in illustrating what the respondents have observed, making it easier for the learner to interpret the feedback ratings and decide what to do differently, if required. It is also a more useful tool for discussing development needs with the line manager or 360 debriefer.

The disadvantage of qualitative feedback is that, because it is not structured, the feedback from respondents can vary widely in the behaviours and topics that are observed, and may have more to do with the respondents' own agendas and issues than the areas that the learner may need to develop. Also, respondents can sometimes be reluctant to provide very specific examples as they may fear this will compromise the anonymity of their feedback.

Therefore, a combination of quantitative and qualitative feedback works best.

Using both structured quantitative and loosely-framed qualitative options within the same 360 framework is a highly effective way of obtaining feedback that is both structured and contextual. With careful design and integration of the best of both options, learners can get a consistent set of messages about their key skills and competencies, as well as specific examples which will help them to continue to do what is effective, and to change what they need to improve their performance.

3. How do I design a 360 Degree Feedback questionnaire that will engage respondents?

Designing a 360 Degree Feedback tool that is engaging is all about using key design principles for surveys, data collection and reporting.

Here are the key design rules for building an effective bespoke 360 Degree Feedback questionnaire:

• Design your 360 around key groups of related behaviours, skills and capabilities (competencies or 'dimensions') that are critical for the organisation. These may already be defined by competency, leadership or management frameworks, or by statements of values and principles. Alternatively, the capabilities may be grouped by professional skills, as defined by professional or trade bodies, or regulatory or ethical standards.

• Within each set of capabilities, create 4-6 questions or statements (also called 'items') against which the feedback will be given.

• Keep your statements short, and easy to understand. Consider the audience who will be answering the questions. Will the most junior respondent be clear on what is being asked?

For example, 'appropriately applies moderately complex learning methodologies' sounds like corporate jargon which will have the effect of excluding potential respondents who don't understand what 'appropriately' and 'moderately complex' indicate. A simpler way of saying this might be 'Solves problems with the right tools for the job' – it's accessible to a wider group of respondents, and is more natural in tone.

• Ask yourself, "Can this been observed and rated?" If not, you need to change your question.

For example, can you see someone doing the following: 'Understands own strengths and weaknesses'? Perhaps a better way to phrase this would be 'Openly acknowledges own strengths and weaknesses', which would enable the respondent to say that they observe this behaviour 'Rarely'.

• Always use an active verb in reference to a description of a trait, so instead of 'is future focused', we would recommend 'develops future-focused plans'.

• Only ask about one observable behaviour in each question or each statement. Here is a statement provided by a client: 'Actively seeks and acts on feedback from others, reflects and acts on own learning'. In this case, a number of separate behaviours are being described. Actively seeking feedback is not equivalent to acting on feedback, therefore it is unclear which behaviour we are asking respondents to rate. This statement should be split into at least three statements: 'Requests feedback from others', 'Acts on feedback from others', and potentially, 'Demonstrates that he/she has acted on his/her own learning'.

• Sentences should be consistently stated in the positive, rather than the negative, e.g. 'Stays on course when difficulties arise', rather than 'Doesn't change direction when difficulties arise'.

• A mixture of positively and negatively stated questions is very confusing for respondents working with a rating scale. If I choose 'Frequently' in response to the second statement above, what exactly am I saying? A mix of positive and negatively stated items can also cause the respondent to feel they are being 'tricked'.

• Stay away from questions that ask for an opinion or sound like a psychological assessment, e.g. 'Demonstrates emotional intelligence'. A question like this can be widely interpreted – everyone's criteria for EI are slightly different. Also, many respondents will have a vague idea what EI means, but may be thinking about different aspects of their colleague. Finally, these kinds of questions can have an implicit judgement in them, and it's therefore advisable not to use them.

• Remember to test all the statements against the rating scale you decide to use, so that the rating statement matches what you are asking, so for example, a statement like 'Always asks for feedback from colleagues' will not work with a frequency rating scale like 'Always, Often, Seldom, or Never'.

- Finally, it's very important to keep the questionnaire short (maximum 40 questions, including text questions), as this will encourage respondents and learners to engage with the feedback and give better quality responses.

To illustrate the relationships between capabilities/competencies, and statements/ items, here's a labelled sample page from one of our 360 Degree Feedback tools, The Effective Manager.

Managing Yourself — Capability/Competency						
	Always	Often	Sometimes	Rarely	Never	Unable to comment
	5	4	3	2	1	?
Sets challenging goals for her/him self — Statement/item	○	○	○	○	○	●
Systematically develops his/her own skills	○	○	○	○	○	●
Leads the team by her/his own example	○	○	○	○	○	●
Asks for feedback from the team	○	○	○	○	○	●
Listens to feedback and acts on it	○	○	○	○	○	●

Managing The Team — Capability/Competency						
	Always	Often	Sometimes	Rarely	Never	Unable to comment
	5	4	3	2	1	?
Inspires the team with his/her clear vision and leadership — Statement/item	○	○	○	○	○	●
Delegates tasks that will help the team to learn and develop their skills	○	○	○	○	○	●
Gives public recognition and praise when it's due	○	○	○	○	○	●
Treats everyone consistently	○	○	○	○	○	●
Help the team to set themselves challenging goals	○	○	○	○	○	●

4. What rating scales are best?

Ratings of all kinds are used in the 360 Degree Feedback, ranging from 3-point to 10-point scales. The most popular ratings scale is the 5-point ratings scale. My preferred scales are between 5 and 7 points, which are not too limiting for the respondents, like 3 point scales, and not too wide that the ratings and averages become meaningless, like 10 point scales.

Similarly, the naming of the rating points can include Agree/Disagree, Expectations (exceeded or not reached), and Satisfactory/Unsatisfactory.

In my experience, the most effective rating scale descriptors are those that are based on the frequency of observing the behaviour, rather than a judgment on the effectiveness of the behaviour, or indeed, the individual learner themselves.

I generally recommend frequency scales, such as 'Always' to 'Never' (as in always observed behaviour) or an 'Almost always' to 'Almost never'.

There should be a clear difference between each rating point and if necessary, each should be defined in more detail so that users are clear what each rating looks like.

For example, here are the rating descriptors and their definitions from one of our standard 360s:

5: Almost always – Displays the behaviour almost without exception
4: Often – Displays the behaviour more than half of the time
3: Occasionally – Displays the behaviour about half of the time
2: Seldom – Displays the behaviour less than half of the time
1: Almost never – Almost never displays the behaviour
?: Unable to comment – No opportunity to observe behaviour

... CASE STUDY ...

Using Frequency to Name the Point on a Rating Scale

We were supporting one of our client's teams in creating a 360 for leadership development, to encourage self-awareness and change around leadership skills. Originally, they planned to use a scale ranging from 'Greatly Over-achieves' to 'Seriously under-achieves', which, although it matched their performance review ratings, was not the best scale for helping learners to take on constructive feedback, or for respondents to be constructive in their ratings. In this case, we recommended a rating scale that had 5 point, from Almost Always (demonstrates the behaviour) to Almost Never (demonstrates the behaviour).

· · · · · ·

5. How do I incorporate free text questions into 360 Degree Feedback?

Free text questions can be incorporated in a number of different ways. They can be incorporated within each competency or capability set, encouraging respondents to comment on the specific competency and questions therein. So, you could, for example, have a free text box that relates to the competency 'managing team performance'. This helps people to focus their free text question or their free text comments on that particular competency set.

Alternatively, free text questions can be used as a 'wrap up' for the whole 360 exercise, i.e. an opportunity for respondents to give their own views completely, with no direction from the questionnaire as to what they should focus on.

Another option is to direct respondents by asking open, coaching-type questions such as, "What would you like your colleague to Start doing (or Stop or Continue)?" or, "What one thing would make your colleague a better manager/leader/team member?" This provides a very easy and concrete way for respondents to provide examples of things that they've seen or things they'd like to see. And where it includes a 'Continue doing' (e.g. 'continue being bright and happy in the mornings because it cheers us all up'), there is always a positive element.

Start, Stop and Continue

What do you think you/your colleague should Start Stop and Continue doing, in order to be a better leader and learner?

Self	I should start to give my team more feedback.
Direct Reports	I like working in Pauline's team as it is a friendly group. I would like more time with Pauline to think about my goals and my career, and I would like more frequent feedback on how I am performing. Start having more honest dicussions about performance - I am not really sure how I am doing and what my career plans should be
Line Manager	Pauline is an excellent team player, being supportive and inclusive within her peer group. However, Pauline is less effective with communication and leading her Direct Reports and tends to put off difficult discussions, leading to issues being harder to resolve. I would recommend some training on for Pauline on how to give constructive feedback and how to communicate difficult messsages. She should continue to manage the project delivery well, this is a strength but she needs to start improving her feedback to the team to enable them to become more independent and self-sustaining.
Peers	Continue being a great supportive collegue.

6. How do you deal with the loss of anonymity when you're using free text questions?

Respondent comments should only be shown anonymously, with only the respondent groups (e.g. peer group, not individual respondents) being identifiable. However, there are occasions where, the way comments are phrased, or specific examples, the respondent could be identified.

For this reason, we always advise respondents or potential respondents (in communications, briefings and emails) that their writing style or the examples they give may identify their free text comments.

7. Should 360 Degree Feedback always be anonymous?

Best practice states that 360 Degree Feedback should always be reported anonymously. This gives respondents the opportunity to provide more honest, and therefore more valuable, feedback to learners. The only exception to this is the feedback of the Line Manager, which in most cases is directly attributable to the Line Manager and visible to the learner in the 360 report. If required, the 360 administration system should be able to anonymise the feedback of the line manager, however in general, line managers should be willing and able to provide honest feedback that is attributable to them.

The process and the reporting should support this anonymity. Coaches or managers who are debriefing the 360 with learners should also ensure that learners focus on the feedback content, rather than the feedback givers.

However, not all organisations use 360 in this way. In Managing and Measuring Employee Performance, the authors, Houldsworth and Jirasinghe, describe how BAE Systems successfully uses open and attributable 360 Degree Feedback as part of its performance appraisal process[x]. This needs to be carefully managed and positioned, but shows that 360 can be flexible in how it is used.

... EXPERT COMMENT ...

Julian Hammond, *Director, TIPS for Good Management*

"Many people say that 360 Feedback should always be anonymous. Whilst I understand why many organisations prefer this, I would not necessarily agree with that approach. Since the learners selected their respondents in the first place, they always knew who had given comments, and given the nature of the comments, most people recognised where they had originated from.

Personally, I believe it creates the opportunity for a healthy conversation with another member of staff that may not otherwise have happened.

My advice to any learner whom may have been upset by comments provided is not to challenge them as being wrong, but to understand why they have been made, as it is the view of their colleagues.

In my view, it's really important for the learner to understand why someone has a different view from them, so I am always quite happy that people know who the comments are from, even it results in a slightly difficult conversation."

. . . . . .

... IN THE NEWS ...

Transparency Pays Off In 360-Degree Reviews

"The success of 360 Degree Feedback in HCL has everything to do with the fact that Vineet Nayar, the CEO, not only 'encourages' (read 'requires') managers to undertake and share their 360 results, but does so himself. Mr Nayar publishes his full 360 feedback to all 50,000 employees of HCL on the company's intranet, and communicates constantly to employees about it." *(Web Link: bit.ly/InTheNews5)*

. . . . . .

8. Should participation in a 360 Degree Feedback programme be voluntary or mandatory?

For learners on a specific programme, for example management development, the 360 Degree Feedback is usually mandatory. This emphasizes the importance of self-awareness, of feedback, and of the need for learning. Mandating 360 in this situation also ensures fairness across the learner group. As a learner, I would find it somewhat unfair if I had gone to the trouble of requesting and receiving feedback, if another of my fellow learners had not bothered to do the same.

Similarly, where 360 is being used as part of performance appraisal or review, it should also be mandated, or at least, feedback from direct reports should be required – otherwise it's too easy for managers to only request feedback from their favourite direct reports. Not only does that skew the feedback, but it can also create resentment from the direct reports who haven't been asked for feedback.

Some organisations do provide a 360 Degree Feedback facility to their employees on a completely voluntary basis. In this situation, what can happen is that only those employees with high self-awareness and appetite for learning take it up.

Where 360 is provided on a voluntary basis, it is worth considering some incentives which will encourage participation by more people, for example, it being noted as a positive in the performance appraisal discussion, being invited to join a learning set or a training workshop that is not open to others, some extra coaching etc.

... EXPERT COMMENT ...

Mark Pearce, HR Consultant, Coach and Founder, A Life At Work

"Ideally I would offer people the choice whether they use 360 Degree Feedback or not, as they are more likely to engage with it if it is a voluntary activity.

However, if the 360 is being used for a group initiative, like a development or training programme, and is going to be a measure for improvement and change, then it's reasonable to make the 360 mandatory for everyone who is participating.

But I do think if you make 360 mandatory, you may end up with some people just 'going through the motions' of the feedback process. The key to make it more than just a 'tick-box' exercise is to help people recognise the value in getting feedback from their colleagues. If they see the benefit, then they will want to do it, they'll be interested in their feedback and they'll be interested in doing something about it. So the important thing is to get people on board with it, rather than just saying 'you've got to do it'."

· · · · · ·

9. How should the 360 Degree Feedback Report be designed?

Ideally you should not have to design your own 360 Degree Feedback report. There are many good templates already available, and you should be able to fit your 360 questionnaire, ratings and reporting relationships into a standard template. If you are using an online 360 system, this should allow the data to be automatically collated and shown to you in a standard or agreed format. Each system provider will have a standard format for reporting the 360 Degree Feedback.

Your 360 system provider should also be able to support you in customising the report if you need this, including branding and look-and-feel. This is particularly important if you have a training or development offering and your 360 Feedback tool is part of the overall package. Here, consistent branding and content is critical for giving the 360 report a professional appearance.

10. What should the 360 Degree Feedback Report include?

In my many discussions with clients and consultants about 360 Degree Feedback, the key features of a good 360 Degree Feedback report are:

- Simplicity and ease of understanding
- Key feedback messages that are clear and easy to find
- Self-reflection prompts
- Next steps and development plan

A well designed 360 Degree Feedback report should include the following as basic:

- Self-review ratings by statement/question
- Top-rated statements as rated by all respondents
- Lowest-rated statements as rated by all respondents
- All statements rated top to bottom (as rated by all respondents)
- Anonymised free text comments

Additional reporting information that can add value to the feedback and the discussion with the learner includes:

- Comparison between self-ratings and respondents' ratings
- Comparison between different respondent group ratings
- An indication of the spread of scores for each question (to highlight any large deviations which would indicate that the behaviour is viewed inconsistently by respondents)

Some reports provide the feedback data in statistical format (means, modes and variants), and in long passages of texts. This can be difficult for learners to wade through and understand. Ideally, as much of the reporting as possible should be in graphical format. Graphs are more engaging to the viewer and are easier to understand than complex statistics. The key purpose of the report is to highlight the main messages of the 360 to the learner or their coach, and too much data, in a very long report, can be off-putting.

The other thing that can happen with complex reports is, when you get very analytical people, they tend to get their calculators out and start to figure out the ratings. Clearly we want to steer them away from this, and towards a discussion about the key themes, their goals and a development plan.

... EXPERT COMMENT ...

Sue Oliver, *Business and Coaching Psychologist, Business Psychology for Leaders*

"As we know, a picture paints a thousand words. Regardless of the learner's personal thinking and communication style, and most people need something visual as well as textual, reports with pages and pages of written data are just hard to get through. You get much better results if the 360 Degree Feedback report has simple graphs and bar charts, and colours to distinguish and identify data results.

I've seen some 360 reports from a financial institution, it was like reading War & Peace each time, and we only had one hour to debrief a 360 and two psychometric instruments!"

· · · · · ·

11. What key questions should the 360 Degree Feedback report be able to answer?

The 360 Degree Feedback report should help the learner and their coach to discuss:

- What are the feedback highlights and main messages?
- How do the detailed ratings and comments support those messages?
- How does the feedback compare with the learner's perceptions, and why might this be?
- How can the learner build on their strengths?

• Where does the learner need to develop, and how will they do it?

12. How do aggregate 360 reports work?

Your 360 system should also be able to aggregate individual respondents' feedback into groups, as this data can be very useful for team development and training needs analysis.

An aggregate 360 Degree Feedback report pulls together the feedback from all individual learners in a group, so that you can see the trends for the whole group, by competency and by statement. You should be able to see the feedback by group, region or function (or other parameters that you choose), and you should be able to make comparisons between the groups to see how they are doing when compared with each other.

... EXPERT COMMENT ...

Sophie Kazandjian, *Office Manager, Stokes and Jolly*

"We always run a wrap-up meeting with the senior people in the company about the whole 360 process and how it went. An aggregate report is a very important way of assessing the process and identifying and examining trends that they can address as leaders."

· · · · · ·

13. Should the 360 Degree Feedback report include any guidance on interpreting the feedback?

Ideally, the 360 Degree Feedback report should contain some guidance in interpreting the feedback, to help the learner in preparing for their debriefing, or in case the learner is asked to view their report without the presence of a coach. However, there should always be an opportunity for the learner to discuss the report in confidence with someone who can support them – the report on its own should never be relied upon as a development tool, without the discussion and support that a coaching or debriefing session provides.

14. Should a development plan be a part of the 360 Degree Feedback process?

A development plan can really help to bring the 360 Degree Feedback to life and make it relevant to the learner. Without this as part of the 360 discussion, there can be a temptation to get to the end of the feedback discussion and say, "Okay great! Well that was very interesting. Thanks very much," and everyone carries on as before.

Including a development plan and goal setting discussion as an integral part of the 360 Degree Feedback is critical for adding value for the learner, and follows best practice. It also allows you, as a consultant, to be able to summarise any developmental trends coming out of the feedback process for a group of learners, and advise your client accordingly.

An increasing number of organisations are now measuring the success of their 360 and their development programmes based on the number of development discussions that happen after the feedback, the quality of those discussions, and the achievement of the goals set in those discussion.

PART 3

Communication and Briefing: The Keys to 360 Degree Feedback Success

1. What does an organisation need to do to set the stage for effective 360 Degree Feedback?

There is quite a bit of preparation involved in getting 360 Degree Feedback in place, but this effort is well worth it, as it will ensure you avoid some of the problems that poor preparation can bring. Before we get into the details of communication and preparation, there are a couple of questions we often get asked.

2. How do we know if there is a good feedback culture in the organisation?

For 360 Degree Feedback to work, there must be a basic understanding of the concept of feedback, even in its most basic form. Ideally, feedback should be something that is discussed and encouraged on an informal basis or as part of discussions about individual or team performance. It is useful to ask the client:

• If there is an understanding of feedback in the organisation
• If there has there been some formal feedback activity in the organisation
• If line managers understand feedback within the context of everyday work

Once you have an understanding of the current positioning of feedback, you can design your preparations and communications around that positioning. As a basic rule, the less familiar the organisation is with feedback, and the less it is used, the more preparation, briefing and training you need to put in place for the 360 to be highly effective.

3. Can it be detrimental to an organisation to implement 360 Degree Feedback?

There are some occasions when it is not advisable to run a full 360 Degree Feedback, either because the culture is not conducive (as above), there is some lack of trust in the organisation (at senior or line manager level), or there is a lot of uncertainty (when there are possible redundancies coming soon, for instance).

In these cases, running a full-blown 360 Degree Feedback may seem threatening to employees. Without trust or understanding of the organisation's intentions, the prospect of anonymous feedback may make people feel less secure in an uncertain situation.

To run a successful 360, an organisation should have a fairly stable culture where people are open and trust that their colleagues will do the right thing for the right reasons. However, in an organisation where there are some trust issues, 360 Degree Feedback for the senior leaders can be a good place to start creating and building that trust.

4. Who should sponsor (and start) 360 Degree Feedback?

It is critical to have strong, visible sponsorship for 360 Degree Feedback, not only at senior levels, but also by influencers throughout the organisation.

We have come across organisations who say, "We want our middle managers to get 360 Degree Feedback, and the CEO supports this completely." However, when we asked the critical question, i.e. whether the CEO and the board were going to get feedback themselves, we were told that the time wasn't right for that.

The message this sends is negative, prompting learners and respondents to think:

* Senior leaders don't understand or trust the process ('so why should I?')
* Senior leaders don't want to 'walk the talk'
* It's not something to be valued, 'just another HR process'

For this reason, we always recommend that an organisation starts with the very top team, making it visible, and sending a message that it's important. It is even more powerful if one or more of the top team members speak openly and publicly about the feedback they have received, what they have learned and how they are working to improve.

In his book Employees First, Customers Second[xi], Vineet Nayer, the CEO of HCL Technologies, describes how he publishes his 360 Degree Feedback on the company intranet. His view is that if he is not prepared to do that, he can't ask anyone else to do so. He also makes it mandatory for all managers to get regular 360 feedback.

Other influencers and champions can have a positive effect on the 360 Degree Feedback results, and the level of engagement with it. Therefore, it is useful to bring those influencers in at the preparation stage.

... EXPERT COMMENT ...

Jane Beirne, *Learning and Development Director, Jane Beirne Learning Solutions Limited*

"One critical success factor for a recent leadership development programme I ran is that I've actually put the head of HR through the 360 process himself as part of a pilot. So not only did he help construct the 360, but he's seen how the process works, that it runs in the right way and that it's a cultural fit. It's also a way of ensuring that the instructions and the positioning of the 360 are crystal clear and strategic."

. . . . . .

5. What messages should be coming from key sponsors?

Key sponsor messages to both learners and respondents are that 360 Degree Feedback will be:

- Important for the organisation, a critical part of what we do and linked to the organisation's goals
- Not just another Human Resources initiative
- Beneficial for you personally, an opportunity to improve
- Not a threat

• Part of what we do and our culture of feedback and continuous improvement

... *EXPERT COMMENT* ...

Jane Beirne, *Learning and Development Director, Jane Beirne Learning Solutions Limited*

"For me, it's great to have an architect for the 360 Degree Feedback process, a sponsor who can talk about the benefits , allay some of the fears people may have, and articulate what the 360 feedback has done for them and how they've used it to develop.

In a couple of my clients, when there has been strong and visible sponsorship, other people have then requested to go through the 360 process. They were motivated by a desire to understand better, rather than feel that it's a compulsory HR exercise.

And in these cases, almost without exception, most people said that they found it enormously beneficial. A lot of them requested a follow up, saying 'could I actually have this process again in 12 months' time to see if I have moved the dial on some of my behaviours?"

. . . . . .

6. Why are communication and briefing critical?

There is no doubt that communication and briefing are critical for the success of any 360 Degree Feedback programme.

Just like any change programme, 360 Degree Feedback potentially touches everyone in the organisation: the learners, who will be motivated to perform and improve; senior stakeholders, whose reputations are on the line and who have to understand and believe in the benefits; respondents, who may be worried about the consequences of giving honest feedback; and line managers, who may be concerned about their own skills and ability to engage with this process.

With the right communications and preparation, all the people involved will be ready for the process and just as importantly, understand why it's being done. Without this information, there will be less engagement and willingness to participate, and even resistance to the process and the follow up activities. Where the latter happens, this can sour any future activities around feedback and development.

... EXPERT COMMENT ...

Sophie Kazandjian, *Office Manager, Stokes and Jolly*

"It's absolutely essential to clearly explain how the 360 Degree Feedback process is going to unfold. If one doesn't clearly set expectations, deadlines and actions from the very outset, one may encounter all manner of problems further down the line.

One needs to communicate detailed things, like whether or not feedback will be editable after it's been collected if, for example, if there are a lot of typos in the feedback. Our policy is not to edit the feedback, even if it has typos or spelling mistakes in it, because it should come directly from the client and shouldn't be altered.

It's very important for the credibility of the 360 to set expectations from the outset."

· · · · · ·

Therefore, a detailed communications and briefing plan needs to be an integral part of preparing the organisation for 360 Degree Feedback.

7. Who should be targeted in the 360 Degree Feedback Communications Plan?

The target groups in the 360 Degree Feedback communications plan are:

- Learners
- Respondents or Potential Respondents
- Sponsors
- Line managers

8. What should be included in the 360 Degree Feedback Communications Plan?

There are some common themes which should be communicated to all target groups in preparation for the 360 Degree Feedback process, whether the 360 relates to a specific development programme, or is going to be used throughout the organisation.

All stakeholders should understand:

- What 360 Degree Feedback is and why the organisation is using it (e.g. for developing leaders, training managers, etc.)
- Who will be receiving feedback
- How the feedback will be used
- How the 360 fits into the organisation's strategy
- Who the key sponsors are, and what they are expecting from the 360 activity
- The timetable for the feedback gathering process
- What will happen after the feedback is gathered (e.g. debriefing, coaching, team meetings)

Specific messages for Learners:

- What the 360 Degree Feedback will mean for them: how it will support their development, performance, leadership etc.
- How the process will work, how to self-assess, and how to request feedback
- Who will coach or debrief them through their report and development plan
- What their feedback report will look like
- What the results will mean for them

• How to accept and use feedback in a positive way, and as a learning experience
• What else will the feedback be used for (if any other purpose)
• Who else sees the output (e.g. will their line manager automatically see their report, or is it up to them to share it)
• Confidentiality and anonymity: the ground rules for asking for feedback and dealing with any unexpected feedback
• How their 360 will fit in with other processes (goal-setting, appraisal, training, development, leadership, management, etc.)
• How to thank their colleagues after the feedback process

... EXPERT COMMENT ...

Shari Khan, Management Trainer, Executive Coach & Owner, Trainsform

"It's not all about the rating scores, what's equally important are the words, the descriptors. Without those descriptors, learners have to guess what the intentions of the respondents are, and what the rating scores might mean. So, when briefing my learners in advance of the 360 process, I advise them first to approach their respondents in person, and ask them face-to-face for feedback saying, 'It's only going to take this amount of time, would you mind providing the feedback when you get the email request?' This makes it personal.

Thanking respondents afterwards is important too. Whatever the feedback was - and you don't know who said what and don't second guess that - I advise the learners to go back and thank all the colleagues they invited, because that thank you is such a little thing but it has a big impact."

· · · · · ·

Specific messages for Respondents and Potential Respondents
- What the 360 will mean for the learners, who will see the feedback report, and what the feedback will be used for (e.g. development only, or used in performance discussions)
- Clarity about confidentiality, attribution of feedback scores and comments, and what happens to the data they provide during the feedback process
- The ground rules for giving feedback, and the ground rules that learners have been given (e.g. not going back to respondents to challenge them about their feedback)
- How to give constructive feedback in a way that is going to help their colleagues

Specific messages for Line Managers

- What the 360 Degree Feedback is for, its outcomes and specifically, their role in it (i.e. will they be expected to do any debriefing, coaching, mentoring, development planning, goal setting, etc.)
- What they will be expected to do to support their learners through the 360, including providing useful and constructive feedback which will be attributable to them.
- How to coach and explain the 360 feedback, and how to help the learner create a development plan from their 360 results
- How the 360 process affects them as a line manager: will they be appraised or rewarded for getting involved, or is this just a one-off task?

Specific messages for Senior Stakeholders:

- Their role in communicating and promoting the 360, and the follow up activities
- The ongoing plans for 360 Degree Feedback in the organisation, and how it fits in with the people strategy

9. When should we start rolling out the 360 Degree Feedback Communications Plan?

The ideal time to start rolling out the 360 Degree Feedback communications plan is around six weeks before the start of the feedback gathering process.

This allows all the stakeholders enough time to receive and process the information (ideally through different channels and more than once), to attend any briefings and to ask any questions, in advance of the start of the process.

10. Is it necessary to provide training in addition to written communications?

The answer to this question depends on the level of understanding in the different stakeholder groups, of feedback in general, how to give feedback in a constructive and practical way, and how to receive feedback positively and to learn from it. In addition, the level of knowledge and experience of 360 Degree Feedback in the organisation will also dictate how much briefing and training is required.

As a general rule, the more briefing and training that is provided to the different stakeholder groups, especially the learners, the more effective the overall 360 is going to be. It's also important that respondents (and potential respondents, where these are chosen by the learners) are able to give feedback in positive and constructive way, even when feeding back on areas for development and improvement.

Specific training in advance of the 360 Degree Feedback process could include:

- How to give constructive feedback (for respondents)
- How to reflect on your own behaviours (for learners)
- How to debrief and coach 360 Degree Feedback results (for coaches or line managers)
- Supporting learners to create an actionable development plan and goals
- Using group 360 for team performance and development

. . . CASE STUDY . . .

100% Engagement with 360 Degree Feedback

One of our most successful clients, in terms of engagement with 360 Degree Feedback, is a multinational manufacturing organisation based in central Europe. Their management development 360 programme has the highest engagement levels that we have experienced and has been running successfully for over five years, in Europe and Asia, and in five languages.

A great deal of its success is down to the company's commitment to communicating with, and involving, all the stakeholders personally in the process. Learners are briefed individually, and in groups, about the 360 process in advance, and are provided with follow up one-to-one coaching when they receive their feedback.

What is unusual is that all respondents are also briefed, and given clear guidance about how to give constructive feedback through the 360 mechanism. The organisation has a 100% response rate to feedback requests and a high level of quality management practice.

. . . . . .

. . . EXPERT COMMENT . . .

Shari Khan, *Management Trainer, Executive Coach & Owner, Trainsform*

"As part of what I offer, I will bring in the learners in small groups, usually of four people. We talk about the topic of feedback, discussing questions like: 'When you get feedback, how do you respond?' and 'What possible ways are there of responding, and how does it become personalised?' That helps learners analyse why the feedback they receive may be difficult. There is also the fact that, if it is difficult (to receive), the chances are that there is some truth in the feedback. We also talk about the fact that, when a difficult message causes us pain, we move very quickly to try and dismiss it What we need to do is just stick with it, feel that pain a bit and try to figure out why someone might have said what they did.

Where possible, I do this with learner groups at an early stage in the preparation phase. I invite them to the discussion saying, 'There are 12 delegates on the development programme, come and meet each other, and find out about the programme. You'll be doing 360 Degree Feedback and this is what it will be like. So think about who you're going to choose as respondents, and who is going to give you really useful feedback'. I will also tell them that, because this programme is about growth, they should choose people who they know has high standards, and who aren't going to give them 5 out of 5 for everything, but who will give them some feedback which is going to really help them.'

That's where my briefings with the learners start."

· · · · · ·

11. What channels should be used for communicating about 360 Degree Feedback?

As with change communication in general, it's always a good idea to use as many channels as possible.

Email is often the primary communication tool, which works well, but communications needs to consist of more than just one e-mail at the start of the 360 Degree Feedback process. You should email frequently before the process starts, reinforcing the key messages for each group of stakeholders.

You should also include other channels of communication, including:

- Face-to-face briefings for learners, either with you as the consultant or someone in the organisation, so that they can take the time to reflect and ask questions. Ideally they should also have access to ask questions in private. Briefings should include sample output reports so that learners know what to expect.

• It is just as important for respondents to know what's going on, and for this reason, we recommend respondent briefings too. This may be difficult to arrange if many respondents are going to be involved, so a choice of drop-in or lunchtime workshops can be very useful.

• Another way to prepare everyone is through team briefings, run as part of regular team meetings, where learners and respondents can discuss the 360. Team leaders can be provided with information that they can use to brief their teams.

• It may be also helpful to provide managers with some training on the use of 360 and what the organisation expects managers to do with the 360 process – this can help them to feel less threatened or anxious about it.

• Whilst the best way of briefing is face-to-face, it's also useful to create short videos to explain the process and show both learners and respondents how things will happen.

• Regular newsletters and updates are a good place to remind people about the 360.

• Finally why not use the company intranet or Learning Management System (LMS) to promote the 360 message.

12. Is training or briefing more effective?

It depends on the level of awareness that's already in the organisation. If there is already a culture of feedback and people already do feedback and understand it, briefing is usually adequate. Training is more effective if you don't already have that and you want to bring everyone up to the same level of knowledge and skill around 360 Degree Feedback.

PART 4

Seamless Implementation: Managing the 360 Degree Feedback Process

1. How do I know if we're ready to roll out 360 Degree Feedback to the learner group and their respondents?

We always recommend running a pilot with at least one sample group of learners, particularly if the 360 is eventually destined to be run across the whole organisation. The pilot group should be Tracked to give you some feedback so that, by the time it is rolled out to the organisation, the 360 has been robustly tested, refined (both content and process) and is therefore more tailored around the organisation's culture.

2. How many respondents should you mandate for each learner?

Generally, feedback from around 6-10 respondents will provide enough richness of information and observation to create a valuable experience for the learner. If feedback comes back from only 3 or 4 respondents, it is more difficult to claim consistency or validity for the feedback.

Additionally, where there are fewer respondents, it may compromise the anonymity of the respondents who have provided feedback. It is advisable that there should be feedback from a minimum of three people in each of the respondent groups (e.g. peer group, direct report group, etc.) for a 360 report to be produced and shared with the learner.

3. Who chooses the respondents, the learner or the client?

This is very much dependent on the organisation and it is certainly something as a consultant you will need to discuss with your client. Your 360 delivery system should allow the learners or the client to choose respondents, or allow a combination of both. The combination of both provides control by the organisation over the respondent choice but, by allowing the learner some input, ensures they also have a say in who gives them feedback.

. . . CASE STUDY . . .

Choosing Respondents

In one case, a law firm, using 360 Degree Feedback for the first time, was anxious about two things. One concern was that they wanted their associate lawyers to get feedback from all of the people they worked with, not just their favourite colleagues. The second was that they wanted to keep the feedback collation time to a minimum.

We therefore advised the client to choose and approve all the respondents in advance, so both goals were achieved, i.e. feedback from the right respondents and minimising the effort on the part of the learners.

On the next running of the 360, the key respondents were chosen by the client, but associate lawyers, having experienced the 360 and understanding the value of constructive feedback, were able to add to the list with respondents of their own choice.

. . . . . .

4. What advice should I give learners when choosing their respondents?

The key criteria for respondent choices are that the respondent should have worked closely enough with the learner to be able to give valuable observations, and that they should have worked with them in the recent past, e.g. the last six to twelve months.

Specifically, learners should be directed to:

• Ask for feedback from all their direct reports. Not only is this important from a feedback point of view, it is also critical that there is no danger of the learner only asking for feedback from his/her favourites. Perceived equity and fairness are critical for feedback from junior staff.

80

• Ask for feedback from their immediate line manager, and line managers or supervisors on specific projects that the learner has been involved in, even if the learner does not report directly to them.

• The learner should ideally also ask for feedback from peers or other colleagues.

5. Should clients and customers be asked for feedback?

This is certainly an option and depends on the purpose of the feedback and whether customers can add value to the learning of the individual.

...CASE STUDY...

Customer 360 Degree Feedback as Part of the Leadership Strategy

A large IT services organisation ran a leadership programme for their 250 senior directors, who are key to the success of the business and its senior level succession plan.

It was felt that one of the most critical skills for leaders was the ability to create deep and lasting customer relationships, at a personal level. Therefore, it was critical for the learner group to get 360 Degree Feedback from their customers. They were asked to contact their customers personally by phone and explain the context of their request for feedback.

Once this was done, the customer received an email with a link to a 360 questionnaire. What the 360 was able to do was give the learners a rounded view of their customer relationships at those very senior levels, which is not something they would get very often. The customer feedback was, therefore, very beneficial and useful for them in deciding how to deepen their customer relationships.

· · · · · ·

6. Does customer feedback require a completely different 360 Degree Feedback questionnaire? How do I integrate the data from the two groups?

There may be some common behaviours and competencies that both internal and external respondents can observe, but there may be many areas where the client is not in a position to observe certain learner behaviours (e.g. delegation or developing their teams). In this case, you should create a separate questionnaire.

Your 360 delivery system should then be able to integrate all the feedback into the final report, showing the combined results in the common areas, and the customer feedback where this is specific to the customer group.

7. How do I prevent learners from 'stacking the deck' – choosing people they know will say something nice about them?

This is always one of the big questions in 360 Degree Feedback, and goes back to being clear about the purpose of the 360 Degree Feedback and what's in it for the learner.

If the 360 is for development purposes only, you should make this clear in all the communications. This should help learners to feel confident in choosing a broad range of respondents, not just their friends.

Where 360 is going to be included as part of performance review (more on this later), it's a good idea to mandate feedback requests to all direct reports, and to line managers, and then allow the learner to add more requests to colleagues they think can provide additional insights.

Your online delivery system should be flexible enough to allow mandating of specific respondents, and choice by learners. It should also allow you to be able to easily check who have been chosen as respondents. The requirements you put in place for choosing respondents should be communicated and repeated through emails, in briefings and at the beginning of the 360 process.

To summarise, getting the right people to give feedback is a mixture of advice, guidance and where necessary, instructions to learners.

In addition, there is a certain amount of maturity required by both learners and respondents in terms of being open, honest, respectful and able to give constructive feedback, and that constructive, critical feedback is a good thing. Learners should feel confident in asking for, and receiving, feedback that might not be flattering, but from which they can learn.

8. How much time should be given to complete the 360 Degree Feedback?

The optimum window for completing self-reviews and the 360 Degree Feedback is between 3-4 weeks.

The process may seem dragged out and onerous if this takes longer. Any less than three weeks and it can sometimes feel too rushed.

... EXPERT COMMENTS ...

Shari Khan, Management Trainer, Executive Coach & Owner, Trainsform

"Communication of the deadline is critical, of course, so that everyone understands what will be happening, and when they need to have all the feedback and self-assessments completed. But there's always this dilemma when planning: do you give them less time to complete the self-reviews and the feedback, in order to focus people on the process, or do we give them more time and let them self-regulate?

I do think one of the worth bearing in mind is what's happening in the organisational context. So is it, for example, in financial year end when you're doing the 360s? If so, are you giving enough time for there to be quality feedback?"

. . .

Sophie Kazandjian, Office Manager, Stokes and Jolly

"With large scale 360s where there are about 30 questions, with over 30 learners, each with 10-15 respondents, the administrative process always takes longer than one thinks it's going to. For example, respondents may be slow to complete feedback and additional respondents may be added midway through the process. Always allow for more time than you think will be needed."

. . . . . .

9. What are the options for managing the 360 Degree Feedback process online?

There are a number of options for collating and reporting your 360 Degree Feedback results (for bespoke 360s).

You can use a very basic online survey tool which will give you the ability to create simple questionnaires. The benefit of these is that they are virtually cost-free, however, they can be difficult to customise, and reporting is time-consuming and requires much manipulation of spreadsheets.

Online systems come in different shapes and sizes. The main differences are that some 360 systems collate the data online but still require you to buy a software package and load it on to your PC or laptop in order to manage the process and produce the output reports.

The alternative is the Software-As-A-Service model, where you simply 'rent' the online system when you need to run a 360 project. This should give you best combination of flexible functionality, and a robust, professional 360 delivery system at a reasonable cost (because you're not buying a whole system).

These options suit consultants, but a good 360 system provider should also be able to offer fully-managed services if you don't want to do the administration yourself.

10. What do I look for when choosing an online 360 Degree Feedback system?

When choosing a system for 360 management and reporting, you should look for, first of all, flexibility. This is critical, because although the 360 process is broadly similar for every organisation, each client will have specific needs and preferences. As a consultant, if you can meet those client requirements, you will be in a great position to provide client satisfaction and stand out from your competitors.

So what does system flexibility look like? Here are some key things your 360 system should do:

- Allow you to easily create your questionnaire using type-as-you-go tools, and to see at a glance what the questionnaire looks like as you develop it. Your rating scales, reporting relationships and emails should all be editable by you (or the service provider, as part of their service).
- Be reusable, allowing you to copy what you've done before and then edit that 360 and customize it for different clients.
- Be branded easily and quickly with your brand and your clients' brands.
- Allow you to manage the whole 360 process easily with a dashboard online (or receive regular updates), without having to load any software on your own computer.
- Generate graphical reports easily and instantly.
- Give you some flexibility of reporting without additional cost.
- Give you the option of generating (or requesting) bespoke reports if you need them.
- Allow you to generate instructions, reminders and other emails at the click of a mouse, minimising the administration for you and your team.
- Generate aggregate/group reports and pre and post development 360s which show the progress made between 360 interventions.

... EXPERT COMMENT ...

Sue Thompson, *Project Coordinator, Eliesha Training*

"When it comes to a 360 Degree Feedback system, we have tried some which we were able to use for one client project, but which were very prescriptive, so we couldn't move around or modify our competency behavioural frameworks in the way that we like to. Because the way we operate is that everything is designed specifically with one client in mind, not being able to customise easily made us feel like we were not offering a proper service.

When choosing a provider for your 360 Degree Feedback system, you have to trust the person that you're dealing with, and you've got to feel that they're credible. You've got to have a demonstration of the system, but you also need to be able to feel, 'Yes, we could see how this relationship would work.'

So what we've looked for and found is a combination of the relationship with the provider, their credibility, the look of the reports, how the system looks to participants, and the flexibility and ability to customise."

. . .

Sophie Kazandjian, *Office Manager, Stokes and Jolly*

"The key thing is flexibility. There are so many different survey systems and where most of them fall short is where they can't be calibrated sufficiently to our requirements, whether in terms of visual format, company branding or the actual questions and the manner in which respondents answer them. What we really value is having a system that reflects the branding of our company.

We also need a system that is 100% reliable and is not going to have any downtime. It's also really important to have someone you can contact at very short notice if anything does go awry."

. . .

Sue Mills, *Principal Client Relationship Manager, Eliesha Training*

"Of course the system must be flexible as you may need it for different clients. You want to have very good support, which is absolutely key. You need to make sure that when you have a query or a problem, your provider is available and willing and able to help, in a way that is straightforward and enthusiastic.

Our jobs are pressurised and we never have enough hours in the day, so if our provider is doing the things that we don't need to think or worry about, that's great for us."

. . . . . .

11. When should the client's IT department be involved in the implementation?

Even where your 360 delivery system is entirely web-based and run as Software- As-A-Service, it is important that you make contact with the client's IT department (or you client may prefer to do this), to ensure that they can check for firewalls and spam filters, before the rollout of the 360.

The IT department can also check for things like browser compatibility, and make any changes prior to the start of the process so that learners and respondents can access the system easily and quickly. Your 360 system provider should be able to provide you with a template for your communication with the client's IT team.

12. What should be done if learners have difficulty getting the minimum required number of feedback responses?

It does happen from time to time that individual learners do not have enough feedback from their colleagues, or groups of colleagues. There may be different reasons for this.

One reason may be simply that the learner has not asked for enough feedback, or does not work with a wide range of colleagues. In this instance, you will need to combine the feedback from all respondents in the report, rather than splitting the feedback between respondent groups. This maintains the quality of the feedback and also the anonymity of the respondents.

In this case, your 360 system should allow you to easily combine feedback from different groups into the 360 report.

There may however be another reason, and it may be that the individual's colleagues are reluctant to give them feedback, which is then an issue for discussion in the debriefing session.

PART 5

The Follow-Up: Making 360 Degree Feedback Really Effective

1. Should I always follow-up 360 Degree Feedback with a one-on-one debriefing discussion?

At a recent conference, someone described being on the receiving end of 360 Degree Feedback without the right debriefing being in place. He said, "I got the feedback and I just didn't accept it. It wasn't something I believed was reality." What he needed was someone to talk through the 360 with him to help him draw out the messages and make them real for him.

Giving the learner a one-to-one debriefing of their 360 Degree Feedback with someone who has the necessary skills is important:

* To ensure the learner reads the report
* To help them pick up the key messages on strengths and development needs
* To provide them with guidance and any emotional support they may need, including dealing with any unexpected, critical feedback
* To, at the very least, advise them on next steps, and ideally, create a development plan and set goals

... EXPERT COMMENT ...

Jane Beirne, *Learning and Development Director, Jane Beirne Learning Solutions Limited*

"I have seen, in a couple of organisations, people who aren't necessarily equipped to facilitate the feedback, and who haven't had any 360 Degree Feedback debriefing themselves, being asked to debrief others.

I've also seen learners who have been given their 360 reports without any debriefing, which requires them to sift through the report to work out what it all means, without any objective viewpoint or any positioning of results.

What happened in these situations is that it soured the whole view of the 360 process. The people involved were still talking about it some years further on, saying it had been a complete waste of time because they clearly had a very poor experience with the results.

You need to allow time, and effort, to debrief and facilitate the feedback, in a way that adds value. It's not just about ticking the boxes off. It's a question of not just doing it, but doing it well."

. . .

Shari Khan, *Management Trainer, Executive Coach & Owner, Trainsform*

"When a learner is in a position where they realize that people around them are trying to help them, there's no stopping them! When they are in this frame of mind, there's no sort of feedback that can be seen as negative. It's all viewed as part of a positive intention, even critical feedback.

For this reason, one particular cohort I have been training have this really special attitude - they just can't get enough feedback! It's an amazing thing to see. They're getting the 360 feedback, they are open to the messages, because they have trust in each other and in their colleagues, and they are really developing in all sorts of ways."

. . .

Mark Pearce, *HR Consultant, Coach and Founder, A Life At Work*

"An important thing with negative or critical feedback is to give people the time and opportunity to react. People need to let the feedback settle in. It's tempting to rush in to put things right when someone is not immediately happy with the feedback they have received.

If you see 360 Degree Feedback as a mirror, what it's doing is reflecting back what other people think about that learner. It's doing its job. If the individual doesn't like what he or she sees, it's not the fault of the mirror."

. . . . . .

2. What is the Debriefer's role in the 360 Degree Feedback debriefing session?

Good 360 Degree Feedback debriefing is mainly based on good coaching skills: being able to work with the learner to help her/him to understand their feedback, accept it, and use it as a development and goal-setting tool.

In addition to coaching skills, the 360 debriefer needs to be able to:

• Understand (and explain to the learner) how the 360 survey has been designed, in terms of the competencies and their relevance to the role. For example, if the 360 has been based on a set of leadership competencies that are specific to the organisation, the 360 coach needs to know this.

• Clearly explain how the 360 report has been structured, how the feedback has been gathered, and how the ratings have been calculated. The 360 learner may very well want to know about this side of the report. Research has shown that being able to show the robustness of the design and process can help the learner to be more open and willing to take the feedback on board[xii].

• Use coaching techniques to help the learner reflect on the ratings and comments, for example, helping them to think about their initial impressions from the report graphics and statistics, what appear to be their strongest and least strong capability areas, and how this fits in with their own perceptions.

• Deal with any annoyance, frustration or resistance which the learner may experience as an initial response to the feedback, which sometimes happens, and help them to get a positive and constructive message from this.

• Help the learner consider their development needs in the broader context of their role and their career plan, and to create a solid and practical development plan, and put it into action with a maximum of three action points.

• Ideally, the debriefer should also be in a position to check in with the learner on a regular basis afterwards, helping them to stay on track and focus on their key development goals.

. . . EXPERT COMMENTS . . .

Sophie Kazandjian, *Office Manager, Stokes and Jolly*

"The way that we tend to debrief 360 Degree Feedback is an initial 90 minute or two-hour session with just the coach and the learner present. At the end, we have the learner's line manager join the meeting, so they can deal with any specific points arising from the feedback. This is a very effective way of ensuring that the line manager is involved in the process, is aware of the objectives that are set, and can therefore support the learner to achieve them."

. . .

"One should thoroughly proofread all of the learner's report well in advance of the actual debrief session because, sometimes, nestling among the feedback, there might be some particularly challenging scores and comments, so one needs to be fully aware of this before the meeting. One may need to highlight any potentially difficult issues with HR or the learner's line manager before the debrief session and fully prepare in advance of the meeting so one can deliver the feedback in as sensitive a manner possible.

A draft action plan should be set during the actual feedback session so there is no need to chase learners for the information after the meeting."

. . .

Richard Jolly, *Director, Stokes & Jolly*

"If there is a long 360 questionnaire, one needs to approach the debriefing session differently, but it doesn't need to take longer, as a two-hour debrief is quite enough. Rather than running longer, the challenge is to pull out key themes that are emerging, rather than going through every point in detail."

. . . . . .

3. What works best, debriefing by internal or external debriefers?

There are benefits to using both internal and external debriefers for 360 Degree Feedback, as follows:

... EXPERT COMMENT ...

Jane Beirne, Learning and Development Director, Jane Beirne Learning Solutions Limited

"As an internal coach (debriefer) within the organisation, I have debriefed 360 Degree Feedback, and the benefits of this are that the learners understand what I do, the values of the company, and how it's going to work.

On the other hand, you get absolute confidentiality and objectivity from someone who's external. Also there might be a perception that people who are within an organisation might be a little more judgemental. There's always an underlying fear though, that if it's somebody internal, there is a suspicion of, 'Is this information going to go somewhere else? Is it going to be relayed elsewhere?'

My experience was that learners did trust me in an internal role, and knew absolutely that the feedback would go no further. If people are confident that the feedback is confidential, then to find out that some of the information has been shared would completely undermine the whole process."

. . . . . .

95

4. Are there sometimes follow-up measures that should be provided to help someone accept their feedback?

Research shows that the more follow-up learners have after their 360 Degree Feedback, the more beneficial it will be for them and the longer the effects will last[xiii].

A key part of the follow-up is creating some specific actions from the feedback. Ideally, the outcome of the 360 discussions should be a development plan with specific goals that are achievable in a stated time.

Even where an initial debriefing session has gone really well, further follow-up is important for keeping the learner on track and focused on their development points. This might be a short phone-call every month, or a meeting 6-8 weeks later. As well as covering their progress on the development goals, it allows the learner time to reflect on their feedback, and to really understand, question and then accept, or internalize, the feedback.

. . . CASE STUDY . . .

Transformational Learning

There was one particular senior manager in a large IT organisation, that we worked with, who was quite negative and not particularly enthusiastic about the whole 360 idea. Her first response to the 360 feedback was indignation: she had expected people to give her mostly positive feedback all the way through. However, in her debriefing and subsequent coaching discussions, she did spend some time reflecting on the feedback, and it was clearly an experience that led her to reconsider her previous perceptions of her own strengths. In particular, she was surprised that what she saw as a 'professional approach' to her work, was seen by others as making her 'unapproachable'.

Over time, following the 360, and with coaching and targeted development points, this manager became one of the biggest advocates of 360 Degree Feedback in the organisation. She said,

'This has actually made me feel much better about myself and I'm much more confident, so thank you for that.'

So for this manager, although her professional skills were highly developed, how she was using these at a person-to-person level had been holding her back, and the feedback helped by making her aware of this.

· · · · · ·

5. Should learners be made to share their 360 Degree Feedback reports with their line manager?

Clients often ask this question. On one hand, because the 360 Degree Feedback is a confidential process, you could argue that that learners should only share their 360 report with their manager (and colleagues) if they choose to do so. The thinking behind this is that people may feel more confident in discussing their development issues with a third party, rather than their line manager. It may be the case that they have issues with their line manager which may be exacerbated by feedback sharing. This may also be the case when the organisation has guaranteed complete confidentiality to the learner, and having to share the 360 would break that promise.

On the other hand, we would strongly encourage people to share their 360s with their line manager. By doing this, the learner is explicitly asking their manager to share in their development discussion and take their development seriously.

One of the most important factors in the successful use of 360 Degree Feedback is the active involvement of line managers in the post-feedback discussions.[xiv] However, line managers need to have the skills and the motivation to do this effectively – as we discussed earlier.

6. Can other causes of poor performance be identified through the 360 Degree Feedback process?

There are times when poor performance is due to process or other reasons, for example, managers who claim they don't have enough time to get everything done, yet spend too much time on the Internet.

This type of issue is not necessarily what the 360 feedback process is meant to identify, although some of the related behaviours may certainly be demonstrated (for example it may be that the manager does not spend enough time supporting her team, because she is busy doing other things).

Identifying these kinds of issues comes down to the coach's skill - asking good coaching questions and helping the learner to understand and analyse what they do and how they do it.

7. Should critical or negative responses be ignored or openly discussed in the debriefing?

First, we need to distinguish between feedback that is critical but constructive (helpful), and feedback that is just plain negative and unhelpful.

Constructive feedback focuses on specific examples of actions and instances, and states clearly the effect of the action on the respondent. For example, I once received the following feedback, 'When Jo supervised me on xyz project, she regularly changed all my emails with red pen – I found this very discouraging.' This described a very specific learner behaviour, and how it feels to be on the receiving end of it. It gave me information on something I was able to change.

Negative feedback that criticises the person themselves (e.g. 'Jo is a poor delegator') can make it difficult for the learner and the coach to know what to do in order to change the behaviour.

Within the context of 360, there may be both constructive and negative comments, as well as certain questions where the average rating from respondents is low. It is important, in all these cases, that the coach does not try to ignore the feedback, or play it down. He/she should allow the learner to express their feelings.

At the same time, the role of the coach is to ensure that such feedback is seen in the context of the wider feedback, whether it is relevant or supported by other feedback. This type of feedback often contains a kernel of useful truth.

... *EXPERT COMMENT* ...

Mark Pearce, HR Consultant, Coach and Founder, A Life At Work

"I worked with a surveyor who was very self-confident (some would say arrogant).

In the context of the organisation in which he worked, that attitude was accepted, if not actively encouraged. This person was seen as being a star, because technically, he was very good at his job. Whilst it was recognised that his behaviour was having a negative impact on the people that he was working with, his managers didn't want to address this because he was delivering results.

The 360 Degree Feedback enabled all that to be brought to the surface. In our one-to-one discussion on the 360 feedback results, he had a tantrum, saying, 'This is all cr**p!' What fascinated me was that, here was somebody who was self-confident and yet, there was a flaw in that confidence because, faced with feedback, all his confidence crumbled.

My response to this learner was to say to him, 'Think about how you have received this bad news.' This was the key turning point. After he calmed down, he started to realise what was going on, to see a side of him that he hadn't recognised before the feedback he had received. It wasn't easy for him, but in time, he became able to adapt his behaviour. I don't think that would have happened without a 360; managers and other colleagues would never have given him that honest feedback because of how he would have responded."

· · · · · ·

8. Should 360 Degree Feedback results be shared with peers, team members or direct reports?

In an open, honest environment where colleagues trust each other and feel safe, sharing 360 results with one's direct reports and team can be a very positive activity and build team performance and relationships.

In terms of Best Practice, it's important to communicate this if it's going to be something that learners are expected to do, and also to support them in facilitating this in a positive way.

... EXPERT COMMENT ...

Mark Pearce, HR Consultant, Coach and Founder, A Life At Work

"In an organisation in which I worked, part of the development programme required that everybody got their 360 results together and then had an opportunity to share their results with other people that they work with. There was something about everybody getting their results at the same time that made it feel like we were all in it together."

. . . . . .

9. Is 360 Degree Feedback a one-time activity or should it be a regular activity?

This depends on the purpose of the 360. Where the 360 is used as a tool for a particular development event, such as leadership programme, a workshop or an offsite event, it can be useful as a one-time activity.

Most organisations, having invested in the 360 initially, will want to use 360 on a reasonably regular basis, usually annually. Other organisations use it as part of the annual performance review and development planning. Another common reuse is to re-measure capabilities following a talent development, leadership or management programme.

10. How can 360 Degree Feedback be aligned with other 'People' processes?

By creating a robust 360 Degree Feedback that is based on key organisational competencies and attributes, you can create alignment and consistency by judicious use of that 360 framework in performance appraisals, career coaching and development, leadership development, assessment and development centres, success planning and employee surveys.

By creating this alignment, and with regular use, 360 feedback becomes part of 'how we do things here', and learners and respondents will understand and trust the process as a key part of the organisation's commitment to improvement.

11. Can 360 Degree Feedback be used as a direct part of the organisation's performance appraisal system?

Many organisations go out of their way to separate 360 from performance reviews and in particular, pay and bonuses. Clearly, a decision on pay or bonus based solely on anonymous feedback will be open to legal challenges and is not recommended.

However 360 Degree Feedback can be a very valuable input into the year-end appraisal discussion between the employee and their line manager. 360 can be included if you:

- Make 360 one of the inputs into the appraisal discussion
- Make 360 part of the development discussion and goal setting that feeds into the appraisal meeting
- Gather 360 Feedback, which is then filtered by a lead appraiser or line manager, who incorporates the feedback into the year-end performance process.

PART 6

360 Degree Feedback Pitfalls and How to Avoid Them

1. Starting too quickly without enough preparation

Many organisations, once they have made the decision to use 360, get excited and want to get started as quickly as possible. They may put pressure on you as the consultant and this can be difficult to challenge.

Most of the issues with 360 degree feedback can be traced back to lack of preparation. The content can be provided to users fairly quickly, but as a consultant, you and your client need to spend some quality time in the design, briefing and communication stages. It's better to start slow, pilot and test, than to plunge headlong into a 360 programme that does not engage learners and respondents.

2. Confusion over terminology

This is another common mistake that is made in even the most carefully prepared 360 Degree Feedback project. It comes from assuming that all the stakeholders will understand the communications and the terminology. Here are some examples.

... CASE STUDY ...

What Does 'Direct Report' Mean?

In one of our earliest 360s, we were convinced we had dotted all the 'i's and crossed all the 't's. However, when the feedback started to come in, and the reports were being reviewed, it became clear that some of the learners had confused their managers with their direct reports, thinking that a 'direct report' was someone you reported to directly. (This was within an English-speaking group that had worked in the organisation for at least 18 months, and where the client's 360 project team had been adamant that everyone used the same terms.)

We were able to reverse the reporting relationships to correct the error, but it was a useful lesson in the importance of what terms to use.

· · · · · ·

... *EXPERT COMMENT* ...

Julian Hammond, Director, TIPS for Good Management

"I think the word 'peer' is another easily misunderstood term as well. We often talk about a 'peer group' which we understand to mean our colleagues at our level. However, some people seem to think of peers as their seniors, i.e. their bosses. This has, on occasion, caused the wrong feedback to be given. I have also seen where the term 'direct report' has been misinterpreted for the boss instead of a subordinate.

I would strongly advise, if you're going to be doing 360s, be absolutely clear who you are expecting to give feedback to whom!"

. . . . . .

3. The expected change doesn't happen

This is another common pitfall: the 360 Degree Feedback is gathered, but not much change happens, or no-one knows exactly what has happened!

This can be the case where there hasn't been a clear objective for the 360, or a clear set of changes that the client wants to see. Where organisations don't have a clear rationale for doing a 360, and the benefits they want, it will not produce any visible or measurable results. It's also a matter of providing the support to help learners make the changes they need to make. The level of support that clients or consultants provide for learning and change is directly related to how successful and useful that 360 will be in the long run.

In a published article on the results of a ten year study[xv], it was found that, for 360 Degree Feedback to create behaviour change, the following are required:

- Relevant content, i.e. content that is specific and customised to the unique strategy of the organisation
- Credible data (from the learners' point of view)
- At least one coaching session on their 360 Degree Feedback

• The involvement of the learner's boss in their action and development planning

• Discussion of the feedback between the learner and his/her direct reports and other respondents

• Consistent policies for use of 360 in other HR activities, including staffing, succession planning, high-potential selection/development, training/development selection and performance management

... CASE STUDY ...

Lack of Purpose

One organisation put a lot of time and money into developing a bespoke 360. What they didn't do was clarify why their managers needed to do it. The client assumed that the managers would just 'get the 360 idea'. So despite attending briefings before the 360, many managers did not engage with the process, and did not seek or receive much feedback. The momentum for the 360 slowed and the initiative declined, particularly because managers did not have to share their feedback with their bosses.

Without a clear sense of purpose, the managers just prioritised other things.

· · · · · ·

4. Poor response rates to requests for feedback

Poor response rates, i.e. not many respondents providing feedback in response to requests from learners, can be demotivating for learners. It provides less quality information and a feeling that 'my colleagues are not bothered about me'.

We have found that non-engagement can often be due to vague, infrequent or plain wrong messages being received about the 360 Degree Feedback, by learners or respondents. As I said earlier, if people have only heard half a message, or no message at all, it is no surprise that they will not engage with the 360. It is always surprising how much work organisations put into the design of

360 Degree Feedback, only to undo all their good work with unclear or insufficient briefing in advance of the 360 process.

For learners, there must be crystal clear communication, from the organisation and on a personal level, about the purpose and the outcome of the 360 exercise. Even for the most enlightened and self-aware of employees, the prospect of reflecting on one's own skills objectively, asking work colleagues for feedback, and potentially discovering some new and unexpected insights, can be challenging enough.

If a learner or respondent is unclear on how the feedback will be used ('Will this be just for me, or will my manager see it? If my manager sees it, could it affect my appraisal, my promotion or my bonus? What if my feedback scores are less favourable than those of my colleagues? Will that affect my career?'), they will be reluctant and unwilling to be involved in the process; and if forced, they will engage only at a very basic, tick-box level.

5. Poor quality of self-reviews and feedback

As well as not enough feedback, learners and project sponsors can be frustrated by many ratings that are all 'in the middle' of the rating scale, or few free text comments or examples to qualify the ratings given.

Equally, lack of reflection on the part of the learner and poor self-review does not help the learner to be able to compare her/his perceptions with those of respondents.

Good preparation and briefing in advance are the key to avoiding this situation. As we have discussed elsewhere, if people do not understand the purpose of the 360, they will not be able to engage with it effectively.

Another tip is to ensure that 360 questionnaires are easy to complete and not too long. The quality of response rates and feedback quality is inversely proportional to the length of the questionnaire; the longer the questionnaire, the less thought-through and considered the feedback will be.

6. Lack of involvement by line managers in the feedback and subsequent activities, including change and development

We've discussed this in earlier sections. The key message is that line managers have a large part to play in the success of a 360 Degree Feedback programme. Whether it is in the promotion of the 360 as a critical development and performance tool, debriefing their direct reports, using the 360 for goal setting and development planning, or sharing their own 360s with their teams, the more involved line managers are, the more value the organisation will get from the 360.

... EXPERT COMMENT ...

Sue Mills, *Principal Client Relationship Manager, Eliesha Training*

"I think this has a lot to do with the organisation not having impressed upon line managers what the development of their people actually involves and how important it is. Sometimes in an organisation, particularly organisations like our one of our major public sector clients, where they are very manually-based and focused on their day-to-day jobs, managers don't think about the purpose of the 360 or its role in developing their teams. In fact, they might think of development as more being focused on people getting out there and managing the teams that are doing the physical work.

The problem is that learners may be frustrated by this, and it can have a demotivating effect if they don't see their managers really buying into the 360. They might think, 'What am I bothering for?'

Alternatively, people might be worried that if they haven't had 360 from their manager, it might be because he or she sees a bigger problem and doesn't want to tell them about it."

. . . . . .

7. Learners trying to confront persons who gave them critical feedback

There is sometimes a possibility that someone who is unhappy about a piece of feedback will try to confront the respondent whom (they think) has given the feedback:

... EXPERT COMMENT ...

Mark Pearce, HR Consultant, Coach and Founder, A Life At Work

"One of the key things that has to be made clear, at the very beginning of the process, is that you can't go and look for the giver of critical feedback.

This has to be agreed by learners up front during the pre-360 Degree Feedback briefings; the message being that if a learner does go back to find the giver of a particular bit of feedback, they will be in breach of agreed rules, and that will need to be dealt with as a breach of confidence.

In the debriefing session, if the individual I'm debriefing shows any intention of 'chasing down' the feedback, that's when I would immediately say, 'Listen, this is not the way to go about accepting the feedback,' remind them of what they have agreed to do, and help them to see how their actions may be perceived by others.' This is probably one of the most critical parts of the debriefer's role."

. . . . . .

Conclusion

I hope that this short book has given you a clear overview of 360 Degree Feedback - the good, the bad and the occasionally problematic!

Carefully designed, well-prepared and effectively discussed 360 can be a very powerful tool for consultants to help clients' organisations develop and change on many levels. As we have discussed, there are some things that make 360 more successful and valuable, and other aspects that can make it less engaging and useful.

Having said that, many organisations in all sectors and with very different goals use 360 Degree Feedback as an integral part of their people strategy. I hope that, as a consultant, you can help your clients to get the very best value from 360, and that it gives you more opportunities to discuss and support your clients in the years to come.

We've loved the input from all our contributors, and in particular wanted to share this final, tongue-in-cheek story from Peter Honey.

"I've always been pro-360 Degree Feedback, given that it's not overcomplicated and not done too many times, so that people get pretty pissed fed up with it - the respondents as well as the learners. I also think that it should a bit special and not something you do too frequently because people just think, 'Oh, it's this again'.

Overall, I think 360 Degree Feedback is a good idea. I wish people did it more.

My favourite 360 story is this one: A consultant persuaded a senior director to run 360 Degree Feedback for his senior team. The senior director initially agreed because he had not realised that he would be getting feedback. He thought he was going to report on all the others in his team of direct reports. So he was very shocked when he realized that it actually involved him as well.

Once he had gotten over the shock, the process went ahead. His colleagues and teams filled in the feedback, the numbers were crunched and the trends were produced.

The consultant then went back to the senior manager to give him his feedback. He said, 'Well, there's good news and bad news, which would you like first?'

'Oh, give me the bad news first,' replied the manager.

'Well, I can summarise this very simply,' said the consultant, 'All your staff, your managers, and your team think you're an absolute tyrant.'

The manager was terribly shocked, because although he thought he was a bit autocratic, he felt that he was a benevolent autocrat.

The consultant continued, "But here's the good news. This is great feedback. You can make some changes and repeat the exercise in a year's time; so you've got a whole year to put this right and change that perception.'

So they 'hatched up a plan' where he was going to do 'managing by walking around', actually talking to people, asking how they were, coaching them and even giving them feedback! The manager then did all these splendid things for one year with the help of a consultant and the whole 360 exercise was repeated one year later.

The day came where the consultant went to the senior manager with the second 360 feedback report. He said, 'Good news, we've got a much better situation. Now your team just think you're a cunning tyrant."

Acknowledgements and Thanks

A big thanks to all our amazing Expert Contributors for your time and input; we couldn't have done it without you!

Jane Beirne
Learning and Development Consultant and Coach
Jane Beirne Learning Solutions Limited

Email: adebeirne@aol.com
Phone: 0 790 987 7525

Clive Bradley
Managing Director
The Development Matrix Ltd
A unique training and development proposition that brings together the very best people, ideas and solutions, key areas: Executive Coaching, Leadership Development, Management, Team and Graduate Development

Email: clive@thedevelopmentmatrix.co.uk
Phone: 00 44 787 946 0241

Julian Hammond
Director
TIPS for Good Management Ltd

Website: www.tipsfgm.co.uk
Phone: 01362 699

Peter Honey
Occupational Psychologist, Author & Management Trainer

Website: www.peterhoney.org

Sophie Kazandjian & Richard Jolly
Stokes & Jolly Limited

Stokes & Jolly is an independent, professional advisory and organisational consulting firm that supports those in positions of leadership.

Website: www.stokesjolly.co.uk
Phone: 0 207 435 5873

Shari Khan
Management Trainer, Executive Coach & Owner
Trainsform
Inspired Development Solutions. Service offerings include: Organisational Change and Individual Resilience, Bespoke Management Development Programmes and Executive Coaching.

Website: www.trainsform.co.uk
Phone: 0 785 569 5049

Sue Mills & Sue Thompson
Eliesha Training

Website: http://www.eliesha.com
Phone: 0 191 282 2800

Sue Oliver
Business and Coaching Psychologist
Business Psychology for Leaders
Sue blends expertise in human behaviour with commercial savvy and pragmatism when coaching and developing leaders to create workplaces where people flourish.

Email: sue@sueoliver.biz
Phone: 0 790 381 1233
Mark Pearce
HR Consultant, Coach and Founder
A Life at Work Ltd.

Mark is an HR Consultant to SMEs and works as a Coach in businesses and with individuals.

Website: www.alifeatwork.co.uk
Phone: 0 208 568 9841

Barry Sampson
Co-Founder and Director
Onlignment

Website: www.onlignment.com
Email: barry@onlignment.com
Phone: 0 208 133 8100

Thank you to all our book reviewers, we really appreciate your time:

Michelle Brailsford
Jupiter Consulting Group
www.jupiterconsultinggroup.com

Marie Smith
SUCCESSMITH
www.successmith.co.uk

Chris Fenney
Training Edge International Pte Ltd
www.trainingedgeasia.com

Una McGarvie
Connecting the Dots Ltd
www.connectingdots.co.uk

And last but not least, a really big thank you to...

Our brilliant Operations Managers, Danielle Bolger, for your help and support with getting this book out into the world...

Stacy-Ann Hayles, a magnificent proof-reader, for your skill, patience and many updates...

And, of course, Steve Walsh for being the best business and life partner I could wish for.

About Jo Ayoubi and Track Surveys

Jo Ayoubi, Track Surveys' Managing Director, is one of the UK's leading consultants and designers of 360 Degree Feedback, Appraisal and Performance Management, and frequently contributes to a number of forums on this topic, including UK Training Zone, LinkedIn, CIPD and the London HR Connection.

In her previous career, Jo led the Learning and Development team for the corporate finance group, Ernst & Young, and worked in the IT and Financial services sectors, specialising in organization development and e-learning design.

Dr Stephen Walsh, the company's IT Director, has in-depth experience in designing and delivering complex software for the oil businesses, healthcare and HR/Training.

Together Jo and Steve founded Track Surveys Limited in 2000, providing bespoke learning and development tools to our customer organisations. Since 2004, they have designed and delivered high quality, professional and bespoke online 360 Degree Feedback to our customers.

What we do

Track Surveys designs bespoke 360 Degree Feedback tools which allows clients to fully align 360 Degree Feedback with their organisations' development, talent and leadership strategies.

On the delivery side, Track 360 is the brand name for Track's 360 Degree Feedback delivery system, which we have developed in-house and have refined over the past 13 years based on our customers' changing requirements. Every Track 360 Degree Feedback programme that we run is fully customisable and supported by online access to information and help, from a UK-based helpdesk and support team.

Track also provides and supports:

- **Track AsCent**: a fully bespoke tool for creating Assessment and Development Centre forms, online data input and instant reporting of results, by individual delegate and by group.

- **Track Click & Book**: a tailored, online booking system that allows an organisation to manage its training activities easily and cost-effectively.

- **Track Climate Check**: a fast and flexible tool for running professional staff surveys, in multi-languages, and across organisations, regions and countries.

- **Track Performance**: get your appraisal system online and make it easy to use and easy to administer. Track Appraisal is ideal for annual and other regular performance review, objective setting and development planning.

- **Track Team**: a flexible and customised team 360 Degree Feedback, allowing teams to assess their own skills and team-working capability, and to obtain feedback from the people they work with.

Who we work with

Our major clients include household names such as John Lewis Partnership, Waitrose and Nuffield Health, as well as major corporations including Ernst & Young, Fujitsu, Saudi Telecom and the Go-Ahead Group.

We deliver online 360's in multi-language versions to our international clients, including Fujitsu (10 European languages), Lenzing (German, Czech, Indonesian, Mandarin) and Plan International (French, Spanish).

Our wide range of clients and experience allows us to take an overview of each organisation's specific objectives and requirements for 360 Degree Feedback, and we have delivered 360 to our clients' satisfaction in all sectors.

We have also delivered at all levels in these organisations, including:

- Senior and board level executives
- Line managers
- Talent pool/high potential groups
- Business development and account managers
- New managers
- Graduate development centres

National Training Awards

Together with our client, Plan International, we were delighted to win two National Training Awards in 2008. As detailed above, we have delivered 360 Degree Feedback to several hundred of Plan's managers around the world, supporting their learning on the Plan Certificate in Management.

The work involved co-developing the 360 with the client, developing French and Spanish versions, and managing the delivery of the 360 online to all the participants worldwide.

Legal and Education Training Group Award

In June 2013, we were presented with a joint award for an innovative leadership development project with one of our legal sector clients. Our contribution to the client's project was to support the firm's Assessment Centres by customising our online 360 feedback software to collate the scores and observations for each Assessment Centre candidate. The Assessment Centre data from observers was fed into the online forms throughout the day of each event, and the results were automatically collated into a single report for each candidate.

Client testimonials

"Track's 360 Degree Feedback has allowed us to run feedback for all the People Managers participating in the Fujitsu Management Academy, both before and after the programme, effectively and easily. I feel completely confident when Track take on a project as I know it will be done professionally and effectively throughout. The Track Team is highly trained and the level of communication within their team means that Fujitsu personnel have the benefit of fast support."

Paula Graham, Fujitsu

***

"The Track Support team are very helpful and always at the end of the phone to speak to me! Easy to contact and quick to reply to emails or phone queries when I get stuck with something!"

MG, John Lewis PLC

***

"Perfect and always immediate support from the Track Surveys team - thanks to Steve and Danielle, great job!"

BJ, Lenzing, Austria

***

"A very effective way of carrying out personal evaluations. Support is excellent, swift and efficient responses to all types of queries."

Aliz Szalai, Nuffield Health

Company Information

Track Surveys Limited
Registered in England
Registration Number 3927228

Registered Office:
1 Commerce Park
Brunel Road
Theale
Reading
RG7 4AB

Office Address:
Communications House
26 York Street
London
W1U 6PZ

Contacting Us

For more information, to ask us any questions, or just to discuss any specific questions you have on anything that's been covered in this book (or anything that hasn't!), please email me at jo.ayoubi@tracksurveys.co.uk, or call us on +44 (0)20 8360 4455, or visit our website at www.tracksurveys.co.uk

Appendix 1: 360 Degree Feedback Basics

What is 360 Degree Feedback?

360 Degree Feedback, also known as multi-level or multi-source feedback, is a process whereby feedback on an individual's behaviour and effectiveness is obtained, in a structured way, from a number of colleagues with whom that individual has worked, and with whom they have different working relationships.

The people providing feedback can include direct reports, peers, managers and sometimes, external clients. Feedback is provided on a consistent set of criteria through responding to a set of statements or questions, generally using a rating scale. There is also an opportunity to provide free-style comments and examples to support the ratings given.

Normally, the individual also completes a self-review which allows them to reflect on, and assess, their own performance by responding to the same statements or questions as the people giving them feedback.

Statements or questions are normally related to key behaviours and skills which are valued in the organisation.

360 Degree Feedback is not an opinion survey – it should be based on observable behaviours and concrete examples. It is not a psychometric test.

What are the benefits of 360 Degree Feedback?

Receiving feedback from a number of different people and levels in the organisation, and giving feedback to each other:

- Provides a formal structure for the natural observation process
- Helps to ensure that everyone is being judged on the same criteria
- Encourages and supports open discussion

- Identifies areas of strength, and areas for growth and development
- Increases self-awareness and insight
- Develops people's observation and feedback skills
- Encourages a culture where giving and receiving feedback is the norm

What makes Feedback successful?

All successful Feedback, including 360 Degree Feedback, depends on:

- An environment of openness and honesty
- A positive view of the feedback process
- A willingness to accept feedback in a positive way, and to use it constructively to enhance effectiveness
- A commitment to give feedback with an emphasis on helping and coaching the individual to focus on their strengths and recognise their development needs

Using 360 Degree Feedback

The 360 Degree Feedback process and resulting report is, primarily, a tool to support discussion with the individual's line manager, team-mates, mentor, or others involved in their development. It should not be used as a stand-alone measure of behaviour or effectiveness, and care needs to be taken both in giving feedback and in understanding and interpreting the results of that feedback.

Endnotes

[i] Gray, A., Lewis, A., et al (n.d.), "360 Degree Feedback, Best Practice Guidelines", Chartered Institute of Personnel and Development, South West London Branch, SHL, The British Psychological Society (accessed online at *http://webarchive.nationalarchives.gov.uk/+/http:/www.dti.g ov.uk/mbp/360feedback/360bestprgdlns.pdf*)

[ii] Vickers, M. (2009), "New Managers: Alone and Out of Their Depths", i4cp (accessed online at *http://www.i4cp.com/trendwatchers/2009/08/07/new-managers-alone-and-out-of-their-depths*)

[iii] **Lean manufacturing, lean enterprise**, or **lean production**, often simply, "**Lean**", is a production practice that considers the expenditure of resources for any goal other than the creation of value for the end customer to be wasteful, and thus a target for elimination. Working from the perspective of the customer who consumes a product or service, "value" is defined as any action or process that a customer would be willing to pay for.

[iv] **Investors in People** is a business improvement tool administered by UK Commission for Employment and Skills and supported by the Department for Business, Innovation and Skills (BIS).

[v] Chartered Institute of Personnel and Development (2013), "Overview of CIPD surveys: a barometer of HR trends and prospects 2013", CIPD (accessed online at *http://www.cipd.co.uk/hr-resources/survey-reports/cipd-surveys-overview-hr-trends-prospects-2013.aspx*)

[vi] Towards Maturity (2009), "Award winning - Truly Global Innovative Blend by PLAN", Next Generation Learning at Work (accessed online at *http://ngolearning.org/courses/membercourses/Shared%20D*

ocuments/PLAN_Mgmt+Train_Case_Study_Jan_2009%20(2) .pdf)

vii Davenport, T. H., Harris, J., Shapiro, J. (2010), "Competing on Talent Analytics: What the best companies know about their people – and how they use that information to outperform rivals", Harvard Business Review (accessed online at *http://hbr.org/2010/10/competing-on-talent-analytics)*

viii Ben-Hur, S., Kinley, N. (2013), "Turn Talent Data into Real Information", HBR Blog Network (accessed online at *http://blogs.hbr.org/2013/09/turning-talent-data-into-real/)*

ix A **'competency framework'** is a structure that sets out and defines each individual competency (such as problem-solving or people management) required by individuals working in an organisation or part of an organisation (CIPD Factsheet, August 2013)

x Houldsworth, E., Jiransinghe, D. (2006), "Managing and Measuring Employee Performance" (Chapter 9), Kogan Page

xi Nayar, V. (2010), "Employees First, Customers Second: Turning Conventional Management Upside Down", Harvard Business Review Press

xii Bracken, D. W., Rose D. S. (2011), "When does 360 Degree Feedback create behaviour change?", Journal of Business Psychology, 26:183-192

xiii Shipper, F. (2009), "A Long-term study of the impact of a 360 Feedback Process on Self-Others' Agreement and Performance", Franklin P. Perdue School of Business

xiv Atwater, L. E., Brett, J. F., Charles, A. C. (2007), "Multisource Feedback: Lessons learned and Implications for Practice –Human Resource Management" Summer 2007, Vol. 46, No. 2, Pp. 285–307

[xv] Bracken, D. W., Rose D. S. (2011), "When does 360 Degree Feedback create behaviour change?", Journal of Business Psychology, 26:183-192

Made in the USA
Middletown, DE
16 July 2016